Lifestyle GROOMING

Ashok Menon

PUSTAK MAHAL®

Publishers
Pustak Mahal®
J-3/16, Daryaganj, New Delhi-110002
☎ 23276539, 23272783, 23272784 • *Fax:* 011-23260518
E-mail: info@pustakmahal.com • *Website:* www.pustakmahal.com

Sales Centre

- 10-B, Netaji Subhash Marg, Daryaganj, New Delhi-110002
  ☎ 23268292, 23268293, 23279900 • *Fax:* 011-23280567
  E-mail: rapidexdelhi@indiatimes.com
- Hind Pustak Bhawan
  6686, Khari Baoli, Delhi-110006, ☎ 23944314, 23911979

Branches

Bengaluru: ☎ 080-22234025 • *Telefax:* 080-22240209
E-mail: pustak@airtelmail.in • pustak@sancharnet.in
Mumbai: ☎ 022-22010941, 022-22053387
E-mail: rapidex@bom5.vsnl.net.in
Patna: ☎ 0612-3294193 • *Telefax:* 0612-2302719
E-mail: rapidexptn@rediffmail.com
Hyderabad: *Telefax:* 040-24737290
E-mail: pustakmahalhyd@yahoo.co.in

ISBN 978-81-223-1150-1

Edition : 2010

Printed at : Param Offsetters, Okhla, Delhi-110020

DEDICATION

This book is decated to

my parents

Smt. Leela B Menon and Late N Bhaskara Menon

ACKNOWLEDGEMENTS

MAGAZINES

1. Readers Digest
2. Health
3. Time
4. Newsweek
5. India Today
6. Outlook Money
7. National Geographic
8. And many others

BOOKS

1. Say Goodnight to Insomnia - Gregg Jacobs
2. The Complete Guide to Sports Nutrition by Anita Bean (A & C Black)
3. "The Social Readjustment Rating Scale," Journal of Psychosomatic Research by T.H.Holmes and T.H. Rahe
4. The Ship Captain's Medical Guide - Mca Publication
5. And many others

INTERNET SITES

1. health.harvard.edu/newsweek
2. www.online-ambulance.com
3. www.johnsonupdaydowndaydiet.com
4. www.wholistic1.com
5. www.brighamandwomens.org
6. www.nia.nih.gov
7. www.nature.com
8. www. wikipedia.org
9. www.cardiff.ac.uk
10. www.Internethealthlibrary.com
11. And many others

CONTENTS

1. INTRODUCTION **9**

- Life is a Game 10
- Welcome to Life Management 10
- Beware of Lifestyle Diseases 12

2. HEALTH MANAGEMENT **14**

- Think Healthy 14
- Be Positive 15
- Humour is the Best Medicine 15
- Empathy is Highly Appreciated 17
- Never Lose Hope 17
- Let in the Sunshine 18
- Lead a Moderate Lifestyle 18
- Various Facets of a Healthy Life 19

3. WEIGHT MANAGEMENT **25**

- Know Your BMI 25
- Obesity from Childhood 26
- Avoiding Obesity 28
- Health Food may be Unhealthy 31
- Know your Cholesterol Level 32
- Tips for Healthy Eating 33
- Did You Know 38
- Food for Thought 41
- Calorie Density 41
- Water Therapy 43

4. FITNESS MANAGEMENT **46**

- Exercise and Calories 47
- Different Types of Everyday Exercises 48
- Walking for Health 49
- Running / Jogging 50
- Swimming 52
- Free-style Exercises 52
- Monitor your Pulse 57
- Tone through Gyrotonics 58
- Smoking 60
- Points to Ponder 62

5. STRESS MANAGEMENT	**64**
❍ Stress as an Adaptive Response of the Body	64
❍ Stress as a Psychosomatic Illness	65
❍ Importance of Stress Management	65
❍ Stress and Body Chemistry	66
❍ Stress and Hypertension	66
❍ Stress and Diabetes	67
❍ How to Reduce Stress Levels?	68
❍ Mind Relaxing Techniques	74
❍ Life-change Index	82
❍ Sleep	85
6. WEALTH MANAGEMENT	**88**
❍ Investment Options	90
❍ Post Office Deposits	94
❍ Mutual Funds	98
❍ Equity and the Stock Market	100
❍ Real Estate	107
❍ Insurance	109
❍ Risk Quotient	110
❍ Thumb Rules for Investing	113
❍ Tax Planning	114
❍ Direct Tax Code	115
7. MAN MANAGEMENT	**117**
❍ What is Man Management?	118
❍ How to be a Good Man Manager	119
❍ Good Communication Skills Bring Benefits	124
❍ Reward Good Workers	125
❍ Good Workers are the first to Recognise a Bad Management	126
❍ Discourage Sycophancy	129
❍ Team Building	131
❍ Brainstorming	131
❍ Advantages of Brainstorming	132
❍ Personal Quality	133
❍ Points to Ponder	134
8. CHARACTER MANAGEMENT	**136**
❍ Character - Your Signature in Life	137
❍ Focus on Developing Character	137
❍ The Original Sins to be Avoided	138
❍ Anger Management	144
❍ Time Management	147
❍ Quality Time for the Family	150
❍ Be Happy with your Job	154
❍ Cultivate Spirituality	154

- Define a Happy Man? 156
- Be Compassionate 157

9. CRISIS MANAGEMENT 159

- Beware of Fire 159
- Cuts and Wounds 160
- Loss of a Loved One 160
- Financial Crisis 161
- Avoid Living on Credit 162
- Check your Paying Capacity before Taking a Home Loan 163
- EMIs may Mean Monthly Troubles 163
- Save for the Rainy Day 163
- Medical Crisis and First Aid 164
- Artificial Respiration and CPR 164

10. ENVIRONMENT MANAGEMENT 167

- Water 167
- Piped Water is also a Scarce Resource 168
- Energy 169
- Preserving Nonrenewable Sources of Energy 169
- Nuclear Power 170
- Waste Management 170
- Greening the Earth 171

11. PERSONAL GROOMING 173

- Personal Hygiene 173
- Hair 175
- Dressing Sense 176
- Etiquette, Manners and Behaviour 177

LAST WORDS.......... 179

1
INTRODUCTION

> *"If a man takes no thought about what is distant, he will find sorrow near at hand."*
>
> – *Confucius*

The concept of lifestyle management is not new. Man has forever been seeking new avenues to lead a better and more satisfactory life. Many theories have mushroomed and many concepts have been tried. But theories and concepts cannot help an individual live a life of bliss and contentment. By grooming our lifestyle we can be in better control of our life and live life by our terms and not survive on the few crumbs thrown to us by an uncooperative fate.

Lifestyle grooming is necessary at every stage of our life. For instance, college students are better poised to face the many challenges of life, if they are in control of their lives. Or in the case of a person facing an interview. A person who has been groomed in lifestyle management comes across as positive, healthy and is likely to be an asset to the organisation. During promotions, a person who is confident and in charge of his life will invariably walk away with the coveted prize.

A question which is often asked is '*Who needs lifestyle grooming*?' The answer is not too difficult to find. Are you happy with the way your life is shaping? Do you think there is scope for improvement in your lifestyle? Do you wish to groom yourself that will lead you towards a better lifestyle? Do you think there could be better opportunities for you if you are able to manage your life more systematically? If the answer to any of these questions is yes, then you need this book.

The fact is that almost everyone can do with lifestyle grooming. It is simply the technique to manage your life in a better and more organised way. Deep down most of us are not very contended with the way our lives are shaping. Whether it is our job, health, wealth or our personal lives, there is always a feeling that it could have been better. In today's mad rush for a better life, we often forget that the main step towards leading a fulfilling life is satisfaction.

Today, life is like a moving conveyor belt going in the reverse direction. If we stand still we will soon find ourselves falling behind. Thus we need to run, merely to match the race with others. This rat race will continue all through our lives.

This book is intended to help you to manage your life in a better way, so that you can be satisfied with the way things turn out. There are no magic wands or potions, its all about understanding the way and learning to deal with all aspects of our lives.

The next few pages will deal with the steps of leading a better life. This will result in letting you control your own life. If you have the will power and the eagerness to succeed in the strange game called life, read on and you will not be disappointed.

LIFE IS A GAME

Many people take exception to call life a game. A game is often not in our control as it also involves luck, but life is something within our control. It is not a mere game, but something more serious. Let us look at it this way. Life is a like game of cards. In a card game, we get several cards, however, it is how we play the cards that makes or breaks the game.

There is a specific reason to why I said that we deal with certain cards? Otherwise, how else can we explain the fact that one child is born an orphan on the streets while another is born into a wealthy family, enjoying all the blessings of life, while the orphan child is doomed to lead a life wherein he has to struggle for a living.

But yes, it is certainly the way we play our cards that determines our life. For example, the child born into a wealthy family may end up as a wastrel and squander away all his wealth, finally ending on the streets. On the other hand, the orphan child may be determined to succeed and may one day find himself on top of the world, a self made and a successful man.

So we can also say that life is not all about luck, but what we do with the cards has a lot to do with what we make of our life. In other words, treat life as a game of logic and reasoning. Learn to manage all the different aspects of life. Every game has its rules and the winner is the person who has learnt his rules well and puts it into practice. Similarly, life has a few rules and if you learn to play the game of life as per its rules, there is no reason why success will not be yours.

WELCOME TO LIFESTYLE MANAGEMENT

Lifestyle Management, or to put it simply, life management is not a mantra, not a catchword, it is not a magical wand that you can wave and instantly transform your life. It is very simply a system which helps you lead your life in a more systematic manner. No one can manage your life for you. For each of us, our lives are valuable, very personal and indeed very much a part of our own that we do not want to entrust to others to run.

My endeavour in this book is simply to discuss the various components of life management and help you to fine tune these different aspects so that you can continue to lead a normal life, but in a slightly more systematic way. Ultimately, we all want to be happy doing whatever we are doing. By managing our lives we can perhaps get a better grip on our own lives and thereby attain that elusive happiness which all of us are searching for.

In today's world we are often bombarded with fancy stuff like 'Art of Living', 'Soul Centres', various types of lifestyle clinics and so on. A number of self styled Gurus have sprung up like mushrooms who are trying to cash in on this latest fad catering to celebrities and thus laughing all the way to the bank. People spend a fortune on these fads before realising that nobody can change their lives no matter what. Ultimately, the change must come from within you, an urge to make the most of this life, an awakening that this is but one life, it's a beautiful life, so lets do justice to this life and lead a meaningful, healthier and happier life.

One day, I came across a magazine featuring a well researched article called 'Guru Chic'. The article was an eye opener. The underlying theme was about the fads which were basically for the well-heeled. If you had the money , then there were any number of Gurus willing to show you how to lead the perfect life and find happiness for you. But what if you don't?

It's all very well for the celebrities to take up a lifestyle as specified by their personal gurus. They have the time and the money to follow the latest fads. Where does that leave us? People like you and me? Also known as '*Worker Bees*', we are the people who are not born with a silver spoon, to whom the nature has not bestowed exceptional looks, body or talent. We have not inherited an industrial empire like the Tatas and the Birlas nor have we inherited a name which can sell like the Kapoors and the Bachchans. Neither are we gifted with unusual talent like Sachin Tendulkar, Zakir Hussain or Stephen Hawking. Thus, we have to slog for a living. Morning to evening, day after day, whether at the office, or running our own business, a self employed professional, a teacher, farmer, or running the home, all of us, male or female, dark or fair, tall or short, fat or thin, have to work for a living. And we cannot spend our hard earned money in plush training centres, fancy gymnasiums or spirituality clinics. And we do not need them either!

What we need is to actually think and manage our lives in a better way than how we are doing already. The concept of life management may sound complicated and perhaps not possible to comprehend, but it is fairly simple. All it requires is to take one thing at a time and try your best. The rest will follow and soon you shall be in control of your life.

It all started a few years ago when I went for a routine TMT required by my employer. I went to the 6th level and was still not showing any signs of exhaustion. The doctor was surprised that a man of 47 years could go this far and asked me "How do you do it?" I smiled and said "A healthy lifestyle". "You should write about this," he replied. That gave me the idea, that if I could do it, why not spread the word and let others also have the benefit of a healthy lifestyle and learn to manage their lives in a better and more organised way.

That was the time I decided to compile those scraps of papers, where I had been writing various points at various times to manage my own life. Keeping in mind my original theme for these scraps, i.e., managing my life, I called the compilation "**Life Management**". It took me another two years to get it ready, as I was not a professional guru or a spiritual writer. I was just a common man looking to pass on what I had learnt, to others.

BEWARE OF LIFESTYLE DISEASES

Today, the most prevalent killers are hypertension, diabetes, heart related problems, obesity and so on. Then, we have the not so fatal, but equally dangerous problems such, as ulcers, nervous breakdowns, low back pains and so on. You might have noticed that all these are what are called '*lifestyle diseases*'. In other words, they arise mainly due to a faulty lifestyle. With the pressures that modern day living has brought, these diseases are always lurking around the corner, ready to strike at the most opportunistic time. These diseases can easily be avoided or in the least their impact reduced by managing our lives. Remember a healthy life is not all about health per se. Every aspect of life goes towards making us feel better, live better and be healthy both physically and mentally.

Most of these debilitating diseases are partly genetic in nature and partly as a result of a faulty lifestyle. Even those with genetic tendencies to develop such conditions can avoid them by improving their lifestyle. It is possible to control or prevent the effects of these diseases by tweaking your lifestyle a little bit. And that in essence is what this book is all about. Whether it is the section on health, diet and exercise, stress management or the part that deals with wealth management, all these have a direct relationship with your day to day living and will result in a healthier and happier you. This is the sole purpose of writing this book, so that society as a whole may benefit by leading a healthier life.

In fact a recent study conducted by an international medical team and published in the journal Lancet, has shown that lifestyle changes can combat ten risk factors which result in strokes causing paralysis and other complications. The study conducted across 22 countries showed a clear relationship between lifestyle and the risk factors such as hypertension, diabetes, cholesterol, etc.

The message I am trying to give here is that this is your life, you need to take responsibility for your own good health and happiness. The road is difficult at times, but there is a reward at the end. That reward, simply put, is what all of us should strive for and that is our good health and happiness.

It takes a mighty effort to run your life in a systematic, disciplined way, without missing out on the million and more joys that life has to offer. But I hope that many of you will try to improve the quality of your own life. And for those who try, the sky is the limit!

"If we wait for the moment when everything, absolutely everything is ready, we shall never begin."

–Ivan Turgenev

So here goes!!!!!!!!

***

2
HEALTH MANAGEMENT

"To keep the body in good health is a duty, for otherwise we shall not be able to trim the lamp of wisdom, and keep our mind strong and clear. Water surrounds the lotus flower, but does not wet its petals."

– Gautam Buddha

Health is always a good area to begin with when talking about leading a good life. The reason being, good health is the key to good life. Remember that old saying 'Health is Wealth'? It may sound clichéd but it's very true.

If you are an average person without any major disorders, there is no reason for you to not enjoy good health. Good health is like a delicate flower. Look after it and it will make you feel good forever. Abuse it and it fades away leaving you with illness, sorrow and despair. Many of us abuse our bodies till it is unable to take any more, and slowly we sink to a point from where there is no return.

At the same time, good health is also easy to maintain. All it needs is a little discipline and attention to what you do and how. Once you are tuned to leading a healthy life you will be amazed as to how far you are willing to go to maintain this and not fall back to the old ways.

THINK HEALTHY

Good health, bad health, illness, sickness, etc., are all influenced to some extent by our mindsets. There have been instances of people with terminal cancer who have enjoyed their lives till the very last minute. Knowing that they have such an affliction is enough to kill most people or send them into irrecoverable depression. But some overcome this by thinking positive. They refuse to think about their illness and concentrate on living their lives with happiness and dignity. Such people are few and far between. In fact some of them have ultimately won the war over their illnesses with the power of their mind, even when conventional medical science had given up on them.

What I am trying to emphasise here is that we should not underestimate the power of our minds. Humans are perhaps, the only living creatures gifted with outstanding mental power and we should learn to utilise this to its full capacity. By this I do not mean bending spoons or hypnotising others, but we should use it for balancing our lifestyle.

BE POSITIVE

A person who is happy and cheerful, tries hard at work and play, looks after his own health, has healthy thoughts and leads a balanced lifestyle, can be called truly healthy in body and mind. So the first step to a happy life is to abolish all negative thoughts from your mind. Negative thinking withers the mind and ultimately takes its toll on your health and body. Thus, positive thinking is the key. Remember, every cloud has a silver lining. Instead of thinking that a door is half closed, think it is half open; rather than a glass being half empty, think of it as half full. Let positive thoughts flood your mind and you will feel the change coming from within.

Do you have a problem which is weighing too heavy on your mind? You need to stop yourself from thinking about your problem all the time. Think about all the good things that are happening to you. Think about the possible happy endings to the problems and devise a strategy to arrive at them. Do not be fatalistic and think that you have to live with the problem. Life is beautiful. Go out and enjoy it. Feel the fresh air on your face. Hum a tune. Hug your loved ones. Try to be cheerful and think happily. Soon you will find that your problem occupies less space in your mind than before and there might even be times when you would have forgotten about it altogether. There is no doubt that whatever is making you unhappy is very unfortunate, but at the same time you are fortunate in many ways and luckier than many others. Always remember the famous quote "I cried because I was lame till I saw a man with no legs".

HUMOUR IS THE BEST MEDICINE

Many people are under the impression that to be serious and thoughtful all the time is a sign of maturity. They are wrong. A mature person is one who has tasted life in all its forms and comes out of it as a more relaxed person. To be serious and morose all the time is a prescription for ill health. Use your sense of humour. Enjoy the little pleasures in life. Learn to laugh and smile more often. I have seen many people who greet each other with a curt good morning or a nod of the head. If such a greeting were to be accompanied with a smile it would have appeared so much more genuine. But we don't. We believe that it would be taken as a sign of weakness and maintain that 'oh-so-serious' look all the time.

Women generally smile when they greet one another, but not men!! They are conditioned from childhood that smiling and laughing are signs of weakness and feminity; so many of them plod through life with a serious look on their faces. They radiate their own sense of foreboding and depression and others respond to them likewise. Such people are unfortunate because they do not realise the value of a simple smile. A smile is like sunshine; it warms every place it reaches and like sunshine the energy is re-radiated. A smile is an investment that you make to get other smiles in return. And it does not cost a penny. So learn to smile. Smile at your loved ones early in the morning, smile at the caretaker of your home as you leave for office, smile at the people who you meet regularly, smile at your colleagues, smile at your boss, keep smiling and you will learn the value of a simple smile when people will acknowledge you and smile at you in return.

Learn to laugh at the lighter side of life. Learn to laugh at yourself and your shortcomings. Do not hesitate to laugh out loud when you want to. Remember there is no rule against having a good laugh. A good, loud laugh drives out the stale air in your lungs and fills it with fresh oxygen. So laughing is actually good for you. In addition, it exercises your facial muscles and ensures that your face remains supple and healthy. But over and above, laughing makes your mood lighter and helps you to overcome the various niggles of daily life.

Humour is contagious like all other moods. In fact, life is like a mirror. If you are happy and cheerful, you will automatically find similar people around you. If you are a grumpy grouch, you will attract other grumpy grouches and wallow in each others grumpiness and bad vibes. Thus a cheerful person will generally have cheerful people around him. Even if someone is depressed, the fact that others around him are cheerful will lift his spirits. When you enter a room filled with serious and grumpy looking people, you can almost feel the tension in the room as each one tries to outdo the other in seriousness. But if a couple of people are cheerful and humorous, it will have a cumulative effect on others and the mood will improve substantially.

Thus, it is necessary to cultivate a sense of humour. Humour should be spontaneous; it should come from within. A humorous person can find humour even in the mundane aspects of life. But remember the golden rule, never attempt humour at another person's expense. The idea is to make others happy, not ridicule someone in front of others. Never make fun of people even behind their backs. Generally people who make fun of others are often disliked.

Sometimes it happens that when you are sharing a joke with a friend or colleagues and you inadvertently make fun of someone who is present there without realising it and everybody has a good laugh. This is the when you should say graciously to the person, 'just joking'. This will make the person at whose expense you had a laugh feel better. Some people are in the habit of poking fun at others. If you are one of them, my sincere advice to you is, get out of this habit as soon as you can. It will finally lead to your isolation. Making fun of others is seen as supercilious and the person indulging in it is viewed as arrogant and egoistic. So kick the habit and you will be a better person. A happy and humorous person is well-liked, but a sarcastic person is avoided.

Do not attempt humour with someone who is passing through a personal tragedy. That's the time to show empathy, that you understand his grief and share it. Let him know that you care for his feelings at a personal level. Try to talk about it, if he is willing, and get it out of his system. Once he is able to talk about his tragedy, he will be able to overcome it, and will then thank you for your support. Remember, tragedy can strike anyone, at any time. It pays to be sensitive to others' feelings.

EMPATHY IS APPRECIATED

It is important to know that there is a difference between sympathy and empathy. Although both are noble feelings, sympathy is coloured more by the feeling of pity whereas empathy is about understanding the other person's condition and genuinely sharing his feelings. In any such a situation, try to empathise with the person rather than showing sympathy. On the other hand, you may sympathise with a colleague who has had a bad run at the sweepstakes but you surely need to empathise with someone who has a serious health problem.

Try to cultivate empathy by genuinely trying to share the grief of the person and you will find that you have made a friend for life. If you are genuinely empathetic, you will always connect with the person. This is because people in general do not appreciate pity or sympathy.

NEVER LOSE HOPE

If you are feeling depressed due to what is happening to you or around you, take time-off for a few moments—think of the brightest moments of your life and revel in them. Everyone has some memories, some experiences, which they have enjoyed and cherished. Think of those when you feel the black clouds over you. You will feel the difference and the clouds of despair will lift. Try it out and see if it works. Remember, the darkest period of the night is the hour just before dawn. So when things look bleak, you can rest assured that there will be light at the end of the tunnel.

Never lose hope, for hope keeps the human flame alive. As long as there is hope, there is life. Once hope is gone, everything is gone.

As Swami Vivekananda puts it: *Even this shall pass.*

Life is a continuing cycle of events, some good, some not so good. But the cycle of life will move on, the worst periods will eventually give way to better times and the day will eventually come. Just as good times don't last forever, bad times will also pass by and you will forget about the worst moments of your life. After the dark and despairing moments, the sun comes out and makes everything bright and radiant.

Even the worst things that can happen to you will pale in comparison to the fate that less fortunate ones sometimes pass through. We are all lucky to be where we are. The fact that you are reading this book makes you luckier than millions of those who cannot read or cannot afford the luxury of a book.

LET IN THE SUNSHINE

When a room is dark you open the windows and let the sunshine stream in. Similarly when the mind is filled with dark thoughts, you should open the windows of your mind and let positive thoughts fill the mind. That does not mean that you should adopt an ostrich-like attitude, hoping that the problem will go away. No! You should approach the problem analytically and do everything within your power to solve the problem. In the meantime, there is no need to move around with a long face and a heavy mind weighed down with worry. Once you have or are doing something about it, be your normal self and do not let your worries ruin your life. Life has a habit of taking its own course and soon enough you will find other interests and move on.

In fact, literally opening the windows and letting the light stream in will actually be good for you. Testosterone levels generally go up in bright light, giving the 'feel good' effect. Further, sunlight is a proven pain reliever. Studies at the University of Pittsburgh found that people passing through depression felt much better when they spent time in the sun. The sun has been a life-giver ever since creation and our genes have not forgotten this, although in today's world we are mostly cocooned in air conditioned cubicles in our offices. Thus even today when we go out in the sun, our spirits lift and we feel better.

This is the reason why in sunny countries like our's, people are warm and do not hesitate to discuss every aspect of their personal lives. While warmth and friendliness is definitely good, there is no point in troubling everybody with your personal problems. It is a common sight to see people discussing their illnesses in great detail. It does no good to the person who is suffering as well as to the person who is listening. My advice is to avoid getting into such habits and be cheerful at all times.

LEAD A MODERATE LIFESTYLE

The best way to lead a healthy life is to have a healthy and moderate lifestyle. Avoid any kind of excess, be it food, alcohol, smoking etc. Eat in moderation and lead an active life. This book is devoted to the ways and means of leading an active life. Read and understand these points and it will help you in your endeavour to lead a healthy life.

Here, I would like to add that you must use your discretion at all times. You know your system better than anybody else. No book, no dietician, no doctor and certainly no Guru knows your mind and body better than yourself. If something suggested either in this book, or by anybody else does not suit you, stop at once. The body will give you enough indications in it's own way. Listen to your body's whispers and take professional help if necessary. In other words, do not take the printed word at face value. Think for yourself before acting on it.

In today's world a whole lot of information is available on the Internet. You just have to type in the word on the search engine and initiate a search to have many thousands of articles on the subject. Remember, all this information may not necessarily be correct or beneficial for you. Thus, verify the sources of such information, rather than accepting it blindly simply because some journalist has reported it or some website or blogger has put up the information.

In other words, adopt a sensible and a balanced approach in life. In all spheres, think for yourself before blindly following your peers in their activities. And think twice before you follow the printed word. There is a tendency to blindly follow whatever is written in magazines, books, newspapers, on the Internet, etc. It is a good idea to think logically before following any advice.

VARIOUS FACETS OF A HEALTHY LIFE

There are many facets of leading a healthy life. Needless to say, each person has his own priorities in life, but the general conditions for a healthy and happy life can be broadly classified as follows :

1. Eat healthy
2. Exercise and be active
3. Control stress and anger
4. Take care of your wealth or money matters
5. Man management
6. Have a good character
7. Manage your time
8. Maintain the environment
9. Take charge during crisis

In brief, life management is all about a way of life, which is healthy. The moment you mismanage any facet of your life, ill health and dissatisfaction will haunt you. The trick is to live in a manner that will balance each and every aspect of your life. This will keep you in the best of health and happiness. And after all, this is the goal of every human being!!!

A short introduction to some of these topics is given below. They are covered in greater detail in the later chapters.

1. **Eat healthy :** Healthy eating is an important pillar of a healthy life. Unfortunately this aspect is ignored too often, resulting in various complications. Healthy eating indicates a balanced diet, regular meals, no overeating and reduction in consumption of rich food. In our day to day life there are many instances where we are forced to eat unhealthy food. Generally if you have a habit of healthy eating, these one-on situations will not affect you. Unhealthy eating habits result in various complications such as, hypertension, high cholesterol, obesity, etc. The details are discussed in the relevant chapters in this book.

   Many people are under the impression that rather than eating and then burning the calories by exercising, a better way would be to control the calories in the food eaten or by starving altogether. This line of thinking is wrong. Food contains not only calories, but also many other valuable and necessary vitamins, minerals and nutrients which are essential for a healthy person.

   By reducing the amount of food taken in, we are reducing the amount of nutrition. This will have major and irreversible consequences later on in life. But yes, one can control the calories taken which helps to maintain or even lose weight. But the logistics and impracticality of calorie counting is so enormous that it is better to have a balanced diet rather than count the individual calories in the food eaten in a day.

2. **Exercise and be Active:** To lead a healthy life, it is not enough to have healthy eating habits. It is necessary to burn the calories consumed in order to avoid obesity and other related complications. Exercise and an active lifestyle are the best options. Exercise not only burns the calories, it is good for the heart and other organs, it tones the muscles and in general imparts a good and healthy feeling. An active lifestyle also boosts the HDL (good cholesterol) levels in the body. Further, chances of hypertension, diabetes, etc., are drastically reduced by exercising and leading an active healthy life.

   The positive effects of daily exercise even for a few minutes are known to all. But still people in general have an aversion to even mild form of activity such as a morning walk. This results in a misplaced sense of confidence in one's own health. Until and unless the spectre of ill health knocks on our doors, we live in labouring under the delusion that we don't need any exercise.

   It is only when they are afflicted with major illnesses such as diabetes, heart disease, etc., that people are forced to take up some form of activity or the other, little realising that had they taken up the same activity a few years earlier on, the illnesses would have been kept at bay.

Diabetes is a major ailment aflicting millions in India. It has now reached epidemic proportions. Diabetes is mostly hereditary in nature, being passed on from one generation to the next. But lifestyle is one of the major culprits in diabetes being so common these days. A sedentary lifestyle, rich and fried food stuffs and a lack of exercise are the triumvirates which lead to this debilitating disease. But more of this later.

3. **Control stress and anger:** No book on life management would be complete without a chapter on stress management and hypertension. Due to the fast pace of modern living, has become common and management of stress is one of the important cornerstones of a healthy life. Unchecked, stress can lead to hypertension, diabetes and heart related ailments. There are number of ways to fight stress and these are discussed in detail in this book.

4. **Taking care of your wealtth or money matters:** There is an old saying 'It is more difficult to save money than earning it'. In other words, earning money is the easy part, whereas saving it and making it grow is tough. Unfortunately in our country, the common man has no clue on how to save money. At best, he is happy to see his money rot in as a fixed deposit in the bank. Most of our working population has no idea of the stock market, or even of mutual funds. Apart from equity, bonds, gilts, gold, there are many other options other than bank deposits.

   It is a fact that in order to make the most of the hard-earned money, every person must have at least a part of his money in equity linked investments. This next chapter will educate the reader on the nitty gritties of the stock market as well as mutual funds and attempt to remove the misconceptions regarding them. Yes, it is true that there is an element of risk in all market related investments, but then where there is no risk, there is no gain. India is poised in such a position that the financial companies will flourish and any investment in the equity market is bound to yield handsome returns.

   At the same time one must be aware of his risk profile and accord a percentage of his savings to nonequity based investments which carry lesser risk than the stock market. Government securities, debt funds, company deposits, etc., provide an attractive alternative to equities.

5. **Man management:** Managing people is an important facet of our day to day activities. Man management is an art and people who

can manage others are usually successful. Man management is not as easy as it sounds; it calls for a lot of understanding, discipline and patience. The most important point to be kept in mind is that everybody has their own dignity and self respect. If the dignity of a person has been undermined, he will react in an unpredictable manner.

Thus in all our dealings with people we must make an effort to respect them. Other finer points in man management are discussed later. Man management is a part of healthy living, because human beings crave for respect and understanding from their fellow beings. Thus a good man manager is a happy and contented man, at peace with those around him.

In today's world, no man is in an island. Whether in an office or in business, it is team work which gives the best results. Therefore team work and team spirit are important aspects of a successful man. Team management, leadership qualities, etc., are given sufficient importance in the upcoming chapters, so that readers can develop their management skills and work to the best of their potential. Not only themselves but they can also motivate their team to work better and perform as a well-knit and professional team.

6. **Have a good character:** A good character lays the foundation of our lives. No matter who we are, poor or rich, intelligent or dull, strong or weak, people with strong and good characters are always sought after and lead a happy life.

   A cheerful temperament is a prime requirement for a well managed life. The hallmark of a man who is leading a good life is his cheerful nature. Keep your troubles to yourself and be cheerful in all situations. A smile, a pleasant word or even a simple nod with a cheerful expression can work wonders.

   Anger management is very important. Many of us are prone to sudden anger brought about by stress, work related pressures, feeling of inferiority, etc. Learning to control one's anger will go a long way in promoting a healthy lifestyle.

   Compassion is very essential to make a complete human being. Unfortunately, compassion is a quality which is becoming increasingly rare today. In the mad rush for a luxurious life, we forget those who are not as fortunate as us and have no feelings for others any longer.

   Many successful businessmen and professionals find that in the mad pursuit of their ambitions they often leave their families behind. Children grow up feeling unwanted, wives disconnected from their husbands. Finally this hard working and successful man realises that he has been a failure in managing his family life. Family is the most important part of everyone's life. By neglecting our families and concentrating on our jobs, we are laying the foundation for a disaster. Thus it is important to pay equal attention to the family and keep them happy at all times.

7. **Manage your time:** Time management is the cornerstone of success in any field of life. A man who has learned to manage his time will be able to meet most of the challenges that life throws at him. On the other hand, a man who cannot manage his time is perpetually harassed and spends his life running from pillar to post in an effort to achieve his goals.

   Thus management of time takes on great importance and should be mastered by everyone. In fact in today's world where the focus is on performance, time is very important. The phrases 'Time is money', 'Time is of the essence', etc., have been specially coined to drive home the importance of time management.

   We admire a person who is a stickler for time and is always punctual. Whether at home or in the office, having value for time is a definite advantage. Reaching late for a meeting indicates that you do not care for the other persons' time. It is absolutely necessary to have a healthy respect time and manage your time as efficiently as possible.

8. **Maintain the environment:** The environment has been neglected ever since man learned to walk on this planet. Till today we have had no respect for tit and have consistently used and abused it. After millennia of abuse, the environment is finally striking back. Global warming, greenhouse gases, ozone depletion, acid rain and so on, have made their appearance. It is still not too late. We should learn to respect the nature and the environment.

   We should all make a conscious effort to preserve the environment so that future generations can also enjoy life on this wonderful planet. It does not require too much of our time or attention. An awareness of environment management is often enough for us to treat our environment as a gift to the next generations and not abuse it.

9. **Take charge during crisis:** Crisis management does not find any mention in any of the schools, colleges, etc. But it is important to know how to act in a crisis situation that we may face in our day to day life. During crisis, people who are unprepared have no idea what to do and often end up making matters worse than what they already are. Knowledge of crisis management is thus important and will come to your aid when you least expect it and most need it.

Crisis management is practiced today in the corporate world, industries and factories where people are trained to face various crisis situation ranging from financial instability to fire. But no one talks about the everyday crisis situations that we face at our homes, on roads, in schools, when we go for a movie and so on.

Most of us live in a constant state of self-denial. We are always under the impression that a crisis is always something that happens next door, till the time the disaster actually strikes when we are least prepared for it. Thus a knowledge crisis management keeps us aware and alert of all situations that can take a turn for the worse and prepares us to face the challenges.

It is a fact that we live in a complicated world with complex realities. Many of us complicate our lives further in various ways. We say what we do not mean and very often we do not mean what we say. But the fact is that it pays to think simply and live simply. Those who follow the simple route to life find happiness faster than those who dabble in various complications.

Finally a healthy life not just means having a healthy body, but a healthy lifestyle, a healthy mind and a healthy outlook. Just pursuing a healthy body and frequenting gyms will not make you healthy. Make yourself a complete personality, someone with integrity and inner strength. Then you will find that every success will be your's and the door to happiness will be wide open for you.

Sufficient sleep, exercise, healthy food, friendship,
and peace of mind are necessities, not luxuries.

– Mark Halperin.

***

3
WEIGHT MANAGEMENT

> *"Your body is the baggage you must carry through life.*
> *The more excess the baggage, the shorter the trip."*
> *– Arnold H Glasgow*

Obesity today is a serious medical problem the world over. Overweight people are spending millions to stay trim and enjoy good health. Business-minded people all over the globe are making millions by t reating them. Excess weight can cause a series of problems from hypertension, heart complications, renal failure, mental depression, erectile dysfunction and a host of other illnesses. Management of weight is not as difficult as people believe. It is not easy either but it is indeed possible to maintain one's weight and even reduce it without resorting to surgery or other medical intervention.

KNOW YOUR BMI

Many of us may be overweight without realising it. This is where measurement of BMI or Body Mass Index will be of help.

BMI = Weight in kilograms / (Height in metres)2

For example if your weight is 65 kgs and height is 1.65 metres, then your BMI = 23.875

Once your BMI is calculated use the table below to find out if you are overweight. Remember this is only a guideline for you to know when to take serious action before it is too late.

BMI	Remarks
Below 18.5	Underweight
18.5 - 22.9	Normal
23.0 - 25.9	Overweight
26 and above	Obese

An important thing to remember while applying the above formula is that, being overweight is not that serious. You do not have to get unduly worried if you are in the overweight category. The category to be avoided is obese. Here again one should remember that being overweight is better than being underweight. Underweight people generally eat too less and deprive themselves of the nutrition that food contains, thus falling prey to various illnesses. If you were given a choice between being overweight and underweight, it is perhaps better to choose to be overweight. But yes, obesity is a condition to be avoided at all times. If you are in the obese category or in the upper limits of being overweight, the time to act is now.

OBESITY FROM CHILDHOOD

Obesity can be due to the habit of overeating from childhood.

Generally, parents want cuddly, healthy and plump babies. Cuddly, healthy and plump babies grow into cuddly, unhealthy and plump adults if they are not careful. Chubby babies are a fantastic sight, overweight children evoke sympathy, but obese adults get no sympathy and are usually the butt of jokes. Parents must realise this and try to make their offspring lose weight during childhood itself. It becomes more and more difficult to lose weight as years pass by. Obesity robs the child of many simple pleasures that children enjoy.

Thus, it is up to the parents to take the initial decision so that their children can enjoy a normal happy childhood and grow up to be normal adults. We all know and understand that it is very painful to deny a candy or an ice cream to a child, but there is an old saying – *in many situations you have to be cruel to be kind.* Once the child grows up without being addicted to fast food, chocolates or ice cream, a healthy life is easily within reach.

Obesity can also be due to physiological problems which are more difficult to overcome. It may be due to a sedentary lifestyle or due to bad eating habits. Whatever the reason may be, it requires great amount of will power and determination to shed those excess kilos. Many ladies put on weight during middle age due to hormonal problems such as hypothyroidism, etc. But they can help themselves by eating healthy and exercising. Needless to say, their medical condition has to be attended to at first. Their doctor must be involved in their efforts to lose weight.

Avoid overeating

A lot of people overeat habitually and end up with a series of health problems. Overeating is a sure way to put on excess weight and controlling one's eating habits always has an immediate effect on the weight of the individual.

Overeating is perhaps as dangerous in the long run as smoking. Both are equally difficult to leave. It requires a lot of effort and will power to turn away from that juicy snack or that extra helping of chicken. Because many health problems arise during and after middle age, they are often related to being overweight, it is extremely important to think seriously about this and take action against this.

Most people think that overeating has a temporary effect and the next day they will feel fine. So, they go on a binge once again. The problem is that slowly this becomes more frequent until overeating becomes the norm. Imagine your stomach to be an elastic bag. As you fill it more than its capacity, it will enlarge, increasing its capacity. Similarly, you will also find that you can eat more!!

This goes on and your capacity to eat increases bit by bit. Your stomach, which by now has become large, will start protruding into a prosperous paunch. Generally the abdominal muscles are strong enough to control the stomach without allowing it to bulge out. As you age the musculature becomes thin, thus the muscles have a hard time to stay inside the stomach. By overeating you are compounding the problem and gradually the tummy starts becoming more and more prominent.

Fatty food is the villian

If there is more fat in the food than the amount that can be digested, it is absorbed in the blood stream to be deposited later in various parts of the body. It becomes obvious that the easiest place to deposit the extra fat without affecting the physical activity is on the waist, hips and thighs.

This is nothing new. In the initial stages of man's evolution, we were all hunter-gatherers, susceptible to the vagaries of nature. Food was scarce and the early man had to hunt for it. Thus the body learnt to store fat so that it may subsist on it during bad times. In fact, this fat was burnt during all the hard, physical work that had to be done in those days. There were days with no food and thus the early man remained fit and trim. In fact anthropologists are of the opinion that ancient man had the fitness and musculature of a modern day marathon runner.

Even now the body is tuned to store fat in order to utilise it at a later stage. But these days there is no hunting and gathering. People are used to an inactive life and eating regular unhealthy meals. Thus the fat deposited is never utilised and leads to obesity.

More dangerously, the excess fat that you consume gets deposited in various parts of your body, including your arteries. Slowly you become overweight and also increase your chances of various diseases including hypertension, diabetes and heart problems. In fact one of the major heart ailments is arthrosclerosis which occurs due to the deposit of fat in the arteries. This builds up until it ultimately chokes the blood flow causing what is known as heart attack. This is the reason why doctors always say that an obese person is at risk of having heart problems.

The cost of obesity

Heart related problems are just one side of the story. There are many other problems associated with obesity, including depression and suicidal tendencies. Obesity has become a major problem in many countries today and more so in the developed countries where almost every third child would be classified as obese, mainly due to their habit of consuming junk food and chocolates.

In a recent study in UK, it was found that a quarter of the population could be termed as clinically obese. If unchecked this could rise to more than 50% by 2050 costing the National Health Service more than £ 45 billion annually. The damage due to obesity is really serious as found in a study by the American Journal of Preventive Medicine which states that the number of years lost due to obesity is now equal to those lost due to smoking.

The problem is that once you are in the obese category, it is very difficult to pull back. The trick is to avoid falling into this category by taking action when you are still just overweight.

AVOIDING OBESITY

So, what is the solution? The truth is that there is no outright solution to overeating and becoming overweight. Many so-called dieticians, nutritionists, health quacks, etc. have made a lot of money with various fads and crazy diets that promise the moon. A typical ad for such a product would read 'Lose weight without effort in 30 days'. It is easy to be misled by such tall claims. But the customer who eagerly laps it up should stop and think that if it was so easy to lose weight so fast, why are there so many overweight people?

The solution is not easy. To achieve a tangible result, a reasonable effort is required. At the same time it is not all that difficult to lose weight or to avoid gaining weight. A balanced diet and regular exercise programme is all that is required. You need not starve, you need not count your calories at every meal, you need not work yourself to death at a gym. It is a slow process and not very evident initially. Thus many people who start off on the right track get frustrated after a few days and either go back to their old ways or fall for one of the weight reducing gimmicks.

A little moderation and alteration in your lifestyle and eating habits coupled with some good exercise can leave you fitter and feeling better. Once you have tasted the feeling of being fit and trim, it will become a habit and you will remain healthy forever. But remember it is not easy and needs total dedication from your side to get tangible results. But once you are committed, there is no better and healthier way to lose weight.

Get away from crash diets

First and foremost avoid all kinds of crash diet. A crash diet will leave you feeling weak and emaciated and is injurious for your health. Further there is a high chance that you will revert to your original ways once you have convinced yourself that the crash diet is no good for you. In fact, studies reveal that people who come out of a crash diet often go on eating binges that lead them to gain more weight than what they were before they started on the crash diet.

Scientists at Harvard Medical School found that children who go on a crash diet end up gaining weight. They also found that such children can also develop eating disorders. Thus it is advisable not to go in for crash diet which promise a tangible loss of weight in one week, two weeks and so on.

Having said this it must be admitted that there is some value in crash diets especially for people who get tempted easily and cannot sustain a long-term disciplined diet programme. For such people crash diet is indeed better than nothing. Yes, crash dieting does work in the short-term and results in a quick weight loss. But even such dieting methods must not be extreme and should be done under the care of a nutritionist. For others it is not necessary to go on a crash diet. A balanced and healthy diet minus the daily doses of pizzas and ice creams are often enough to remain fit and healthy.

You do not need fads and fancies

Some eminent dieticians have come out with a low-fat high-carb diet, while others suggest a low-carb normal-fat diet. Some swear by a low fat, low-carb diet. A recent study suggests a Low Glycemic diet which is supposed to lead to weight loss. Ultimately the whole issue becomes so complicated that it is beyond the comprehension of the ordinary man. Most of us cannot afford the luxury of dietician-supervised meals. So people who start on one or the other of these fancy diets usually give up after some time and get on with their lives. As the old saying goes it is relatively easy to lose weight, but much harder to keep it down.

Two of the latest fads to hit the town are Detox diets and Hypoxi-therapy. There appears to be a demand for such exotic treatment amongst the well heeled.

Detox diets are ideally done under the advice of a diet consultant or a nutritionist. It includes eliminating certain unhealthy food while including some healthy ones to help the body rid itself of toxic materials. Oils, fried food, meats, etc., are reduced while the intake of fruits, vegetables, nuts, etc., are increased. Fluid intake is also increased. The net effect is to detoxify the system. Although detox diets are reasonably effective, you do not have to pay a fancy amount to a diet consultant to achieve the same result. Any reasonable human being is able to judge for himself what sorts of food is harmful and which are not. If we allow our minds to work and follow it's advice, we can automatically reduce the intake of food stuffs which are known to be harmful for the body.

Hypoxi is targeted body shaping that ensures sufficient blood circulation to fat deposits during a cardio-training programme. It is a machine which you have to enter and start the requisite exercise programme under a trainer. The machine creates a vacuum that directs the blood to the fatty tissues and thereby helps to burn them. Thus during the workout the weight loss is speeded up and takes place from specific areas where the fat has been deposited. It is an expensive treatment and is obviously meant for those with money to spare. There are other ways to lose weight as specified in the section on exercises which are easier on the wallet and give better cardio-protection and muscle toning.

Then there are a whole lot of products out there which are long on promises, but short on results. Hunger reducing tablets, meal replacement biscuits, formula shakes, various sorts of herbal teas and many other such products to dazzle the weight watcher. These may be effective as long as you continue with the programme. But you cannot continue having meal replacement tablets and formulas for a lifetime. Once you stop having these fancy products, you start putting on weight once more.

And very importantly they lighten your wallet faster than your weight. Meal replacement products have side effects such as, headache, fatigue, irritability and dizziness, amongst others. Some of them even cause hormonal imbalances which can have irreversible consequences. Ultimately it is important to remember that it is your health that you are playing around with. No doubt, it is more difficult to lose weight the conventional way, i.e., by a controlled diet and exercise, but believe me these will reap rich rewards for you all your life.

Don't fall for gimmicks and sales talks

How do these gimmicks work? They give you an initial feeling of losing weight, which can be dangerous in the long run. For example, there are some herbal supplements available in the market which promise weight loss in excess of 10 kilos in one month. Many of these contain diuretics and laxatives, wherein the user may notice an initial dip in his weight due to water loss. But unfortunately fat cannot be flushed out like water and the lost weight is soon gained back.

Overweight people are thus often victims of hard selling tactics by unscrupulous companies. Many slimming centres dress up their consultants in white uniforms to give a feeling of authenticity and purity. Diet formulas are routed through pharmacies to give an image of respectability. Nowadays with the advent of the Internet, it is possible to sell such products without having much of an infrastructure. Good marketing can often help these companies make a tidy sum before people realise the ineffectiveness of such formulas. Unfortunately too many people prefer to take the easy way out. They try to reduce their weight through these gimmicks before getting frustrated and resigning themselves to a life of being overweight. It is unfortunate because it need not be this way.

The latest in this list of fads is called a gastric bypass which involves restricting food intake thus resulting in loss of weight. A gastric bypass essentially is a means of bypassing the stomach, so that the patient cannot consume much food. The common way to achieve this is to either staple a part of the stomach or surgically remove a part. It works by reducing the space in the stomach, so that one feels full after having a small amount of food. But the problem is that once you go for this you remain a patient for life. Once you have taken recourse to the gastric bypass, you can never enjoy the taste of a good meal, never eat what you want and never, ever indulge. People who undergo this treatment often have the tendency to vomit after a meal, because what's left of their stomach cannot take in the food they try to eat. This treatment is supposed to be only for those with medical problems caused due to obesity. But unscrupulous players often play around with the rules for their own monetary gain and sell this as a cosmetic treatment. In fact a gastric bypass deprives the body of valuable vitamins and nutrients many of which cannot be substituted by pills, with the result that the patient suffers in the long run.

In case you still want to try one of these fads it is a good idea to consult your doctor. Your doctor is the right person, well qualified to decide whether any of these treatments are suitable for you. Nine out of ten times the doctor will warn you against any of these fads. Only if you are clinically obese, will a doctor suggest extraneous means to reduce weight. In all other cases the sensible solution is simply some good calorie burning activity and the will to say 'No' to overeating and junk food.

HEALTH FOOD MAY BE UNHEALTHY

Be careful of the so-called health foods that are available freely these days. Although these so-called light food may not always be injurious for health, they generally do not have much effect unless you have the will power to moderate your diet, in which case you do not need to take recourse to such stuffs anyway. And there have been cases where these so-called health foods from fly-by-night companies have had various side effects which have resulted in serious complications.

So what am I trying to say? Simply this, be careful, think ten times before you plunge into any short-cut method for weight reduction. Not only could it be ineffective and expensive, it could also ruin your health further. The fact is, you do not need to get into any fad to get rid of those excess kilos. All you need is to understand what makes you put on weight and a little bit of will power to say those all important words to yourself "Enough is enough". It is important to know that the power to be fit and healthy rests with you and not in some gimmicks which could do you more harm than good. There is no well wisher for you better than yourself, so you have to take an informed decision and decide to get back to healthy eating and living habits. You need information, determination and the will power to stick to your routine even if you find that the results are slow.

Here I would like to once again emphasise on an important point. Never go for starvation. Eating much less than what your body requires will deprive your system of essential nutrients and vitamins, the absence of which can lead to long-term irreversible damage. The idea is to neither eat more nor eat less. No one can tell you what is more for you and what is less. You have to decide for yourself and eat just what is enough for your body. If you learn to listen to the signals your body sends you, you will generally neither overeat nor starve.

KNOW YOUR CHOLESTEROL LEVEL

One of the early signs of unhealthy eating leading to possible trouble ahead is the cholesterol content in the blood. Cholesterol is a wax like substance found in the blood. If the cholesterol level in the blood exceeds the normal requirement, it is deposited along the walls of the arteries and is known as plaque. This narrows the arteries and can lead to serious heart diseases. This condition, known as atherosclerosis, limits the flow of blood and causes angina pain. Further it can trigger the formation of a clot causing coronary thrombosis which stops the flow of blood causing heart attack. High cholesterol can be avoided by regular exercise and dietary control.

There are two types of cholesterol – LDL and HDL. LDL cholesterol is the bad cholesterol because it is deposited along the arterial walls. HDL cholesterol is considered to be good cholesterol because it transports the cholesterol back to the liver where it is secreted in the bile. The best way to reduce LDL and increase HDL cholesterol is by healthy eating and exercise.

It is a good practice to go for a lipid profile checkup once a year especially for those over forty years of age. This checks the cholesterol as well as the triglycerides in the blood. Any Doctor will be able to read these reports and prescribe the necessary medication in case you are above the limits.

But remember the old adage "*Prevention is better than cure*". So no matter what age you are, the time to start on a prevention programme is now. Eat healthy, live healthy and you can rest assured that your health will not desert you for many years to come.

Restrain your Urge to Eat

The best part is that your body is always with you and eager to assist you in every manner to lead a controlled life. Once you reduce your intake of rich food and keep clear of junk food, you will notice that your urge for such food will diminish over time. It is only during the first few days that you will have a strong desire to get back to the old ways. But once you have decided and have started a health programme you will find that maintaining it will become easier as you go along.

For example, people who are obese, will find that if they control their urge to over-eat they will reduce in a matter of days. This is because the stomach will automatically shrink somewhat to cope with the reduced food intake and your uncontrollable hunger pangs will die down. This is a cycle which, once started in earnest, will lead you to a better and healthier you. Similarly once you lay-off junk food, even the sight of such food will send shivers down your spine and your body will reject such food.

This is the solution you must aim for and believe me it is not difficult at all. It just needs a firm start and soon you will find that your body will respond by staying fit and healthy and will warn you if you stray.

I would like to add an important rider here. Clinically obese people require medical help. Those already in the obese category need urgent treatment if they are not to suffer severe damage to their organs. Obesity may not always be due to over-eating or sedentary lifestyle but also due to medical problems such as hormonal imbalances, depression or simply genetic in nature. To these people my request is to consult a doctor and start medical treatment immediately.

TIPS FOR HEALTHY EATING

Remember the following points to maintain good health :

1. You do not need fads or diets; what you need is a commonsense approach towards life in general.
2. Eat in moderation. No matter what the occasion, no matter who forces you to overeat, remember your health is your own concern. Be confident and have the courage to refuse politely. You must never

eat until you are completely full in the stomach. Stop before your body gives you the signal of fullness, because by then it is already too late. It takes almost 20 minutes for the brain to signal that you have had enough. So if you wait for that signal, you are overeating. Eat 75% of your full capacity. This leads to a complicated situation as by the time you get the feeling of fullness and stop eating, it is already too late. This can be overcome by knowing what quantity makes you full and eating 75% of this known quantity. This way you will never have the feeling of fullness and subsequently no danger of overeating.

3. Avoid rich food. Rich food contains lots of cholesterol, fats and carbohydrates. Thus when you find that the food on your plate is too rich, eat half of what you would normally eat. Food served on ceremonial occasions is generally rich and should be eaten with caution. Anyone who goes on a binge on such occasions will have a miserable night and if done too often can have long-term ill-effects. Most food served on these occasions is necessarily rich because substances such as cashewnuts, butter, cheese, fats, oils, etc., are added in excess in order to make the food tastier. Remember rich food gives a double blow to the system. Due to the high content of fats and oil they are difficult to digest and cause indigestion. Secondly, the digested fats and oil go straight where they cause maximum harm - lining the arteries, leading to heart diseases and as body fat increases your BMI and ultimately causes obesity. These effects which may arise within a short period may take years to reduce. Hence rich food should not be taken consistently or on a daily basis. Always eat half your normal amount if the food is rich.

4. Eat lots of vegetables. Vegetables are a rich source of vitamins and fibre, at the same time they contain less carbohydrates and practically no fat. Vegetables also contain lots of vitamins and minerals which are not found in meat. Fibre is good for digestion and keeps the system in good condition. A high fibre diet not only reduces the amount of fats and carbohydrates in your diet, it also ensures a good motions.

5. Many doctors recommend a diet high in vegetables, fruits and low fat dairy products. This type of diet has been proved to reduce blood pressure and prevent heart disease. The latest studies in Japan have proved that this is due to the fact that such diet acts as a diuretic, increasing the removal of salt from the body. When the salt content in our bloodstream reduces, the blood viscosity also reduces, i.e., the blood becomes thinner and the blood pressure drops. In fact diuretics are known to protect the heart better than other medication.

6. Leafy vegetables contain folate which is a necessary nutrient for the body since folate also helps in overcoming depression.
7. Take a leaf out of Popeye's book. Eat spinach. Not only is spinach a leafy vegetable, having all the inherent good qualities associated therein, it is reported to reduce the risk of macular degeneration, which causes blindness in the elderly.
8. Eat fibrous food. It is well-known that a high-fibre diet provides considerable protection from heart disease and helps in weight reduction. This may be due to three factors. First, the fibre itself may provide some sort of protection, second since a high fibre diet includes more grains, fruits and vegetables which by themselves have protective factors, and third because a high fibre diet is essentially low in fat. Recent studies in Finland have established that the main heart protection comes from the fibre itself. Thus it is established beyond doubt that a high fibre diet is indeed good for the heart. In other words eating more fibrous food such as vegetables, grains and fruits will help.
9. All carbohydrates are not to be avoided. It is the type of carbohydrates that is important. You must eat complex carbohydrates and avoid white, sugary stuff, cakes, cookies, etc. Beans are a great source of complex carbohydrates, as is brown rice, whole grains and most vegetables.
10. Similarly, all fats are not bad. Avoid the hydrogenated fats (liquid vegetable oils in solid form), trans-fats (partially hydrogenated vegetable oils found in crispy snacks and fried fast food) and the fats found in meat. But it is important to remember here that fats contribute to the taste of the food and if the fat is totally cut back the taste suffers and it becomes very difficult to stay on diet. Thus people who try hard soon give up and accept defeat.
11. Eat less meat. Meat contains proteins which are necessary for tissue and muscle building. Thus as you grow older the requirement of proteins reduces. At the same time meat contains saturated fat which leads to the rise in blood cholesterol level. Thus many dieticians recommend no more than three to four servings of meat per week.
12. Eat fish, if you are a non-vegetarian. Fish is one of the best fat free proteins available. Ocean fish contains iodine which is necessary for our body. Most fishes also are a source of omega-3 fatty acids which reduces the risk of heart disease. For those without heart disease, two servings of fish per week is said to be enough for their intake of omega-3 fatty acids. Naturally people with a heart disease will need supplements along with their diet, which will be recommended by their doctor.

13. Avoid junk food at all cost. Junk food usually contains trans-fats which is found in crispy snacks and fried fast food. Weaning yourself away from those delectable snacks and fried stuff will go a long away towards improving your health. In fact junk food contains no appreciable nutrients or vitamins. Thus, it is a lose-lose situation where you consume hardly anything of use for the body, but good amount of harmful stuff. In addition, most junk food contains great amount of salt which can be very harmful for those with traces of hypertension. In short, junk food is the curse of the modern era and the further you stay away from it, the better for your health.

14. Do not drink too much water during a meal. Water during a meal dilutes the digestive juices and your digestion will suffer as a result. Drinking water also prevents the fats from being broken down and as a result they are absorbed into the blood stream. Thus drink just enough water to hydrate the food to make it easier to swallow. Many people are in the habit of gulping down glassfuls of water during meals. This habit needs to be done away with and only limited amount of water should be drunk during meals. Water should be drunk half an hour before and after every meal.

15. Drink tea rather than coffee or soft drinks. Tea is generally good for health. Tea contains antioxidants which prevents diseases to a certain extent. All types of tea - Green, Black and Oolong have various properties which help our system. A research conducted at the Brigham and Women's Hospital in Boston found evidence that drinking tea boosts the immune system. Remember tea taken without milk is more potent and also the absence of milk means that much lesser calories for you to burn off! Coffee on the other hand contains caffeine which is a stimulant. But it is harmful in the long run. Similarly, aerated and cola-based drinks contain sugar and other chemicals which are not conducive to good health.

16. Cinnamon has been found to reduce blood sugar. Researchers at the US Department of Agriculture found that daily intake of just half a teaspoon of cinnamon reduces total cholesterol, bad cholesterol and triglycerides by upto 30 percent in a study of people with type 2 diabetes. So for diabetic patients a cinnamon stick in their tea might be of help. It is also known to be an effective breath purifier as it kills bacteria in the mouth which causes bad breath. However, some people may be allergic to cinnamon so it is better to check before consumption.

    However, it is cautioned that cinnamon should not be ingested consistently over longer periods of time since table cinnamon compounds may accumulate in the body.

17. Consume garlic in some form or the other. Garlic helps in reducing cholesterol, at the same time it is known to kill viruses. Thus it helps our system to overcome viral infections. But remember it can be the cause of bad breath. Garlic pearls are easily available in Chemist shops and can be consumed instead of raw garlic. This way you can avoid the pungent taste, at the same time avoid the bad breath too. Garlic is best if eaten in the morning in an empty stomach. But be sure to drink at least two glasses of water in the morning before eating garlic. This will reduce any chances of acidity. Brush your teeth only after eating the garlic just to ensure that bad breath does not plague you.

18. Eat regular meals. If you eat at regular times, your system will be prepared for it and your digestion will be a whole lot better. Avoid eating at irregular times. Unfortunately most people are unable to eat at regular times due to travel schedules, business meetings or overload of work in the office. But if eating at irregular times becomes a habit, then your health is going to deteriorate. Thus eating regular meals is an important factor for good health.

19. Avoid jumbo-size meals, instead, eat snack-size meals. In case you feel hungry after four to five hours have another snack size meal. You will feel lighter and more energetic, your digestive system will thank you for it and you will be able to control that tummy better if there is less food in it. In short, we simply do not need very large quantities of food every day. If you are one of those who eat well, it could be a good idea to cut down on the quantities gradually.

20. The urge to have better eating habits must come from within you. Nobody can force you to eat only as much as you need. Educate yourself. Read about the nutrients that food contains, in order to get a good idea of what is good for you and what is not. That effort must come from within you. Once you know the different food types and understand the various effects it has on your system, it will be easier for you to control yourself without harming your system by going on diet.

21. You must remember that all fruits and fruit juices are rich in carbohydrates due to their high sugar content and thus should be consumed to a limit. In addition fruit juices lack the fibre content of fruit and thus avoided.

22. Chicken breast is leaner than chicken wings and legs. So let go of that juicy leg piece and settle instead for the bony breast piece if you want to lose weight.

23. Reduce your intake of potatoes. There is no study to prove that the good effects of potatoes overrides its high carbohydrate content. Sweet potatoes, white potatoes, yams, corns, pasta, pastries, etc.,

should all go into your little black book as items to be controlled, but not avoided altogether.

24. Have less of rice and chapattis. One bowl of rice or one or two chapattis should be enough for a meal. Substitute with vegetables.

25. It has now been established that eggs are not the villains that they were previously believed to be. One egg a day is perfectly alright for a healthy individual. People with heart conditions and high cholesterol level should avoid eating the yolk and have only the whites.

26. Try to eat your meals at home. Home cooked food is much more nutritious and less harmful than hotel food. Eating out once in a while is acceptable, but no more than that.

27. Have fun. Eat with your family and loved ones. It is a proven fact that food eaten when one is happy is better digested than that eaten in a sombre atmosphere. Music during meal times is a great stress buster and will be of good help. In fact a good environment during meal times is a great positive not only for the health but for the family as a whole. Make meal times with your family an enjoyable experience and you will find that your family life shows a marked improvement.

28. Remember, in order to reduce weight it is not necessary to diet, it is enough to develop better eating habits, to be more choosy as to what you eat and what you don't. And exercise!!

29. Always consult your doctor or family physician before you start a new diet or try anything new, as every individual is unique and your doctor knows your physiology best.

DID YOU KNOW

1. Drinking a glass or two of red wine reduces the risk of heart disease and cancer. Australian scientist, David Sinclair working at Harvard Medical school has found that resveratrol, a compound in red grapes turns on the enzyme that controls ageing in living beings - thus slowing down the ageing process and delaying age-related illnesses. But generally doctors never recommend the consumption of alcohol, because they do not want to give a green signal to alcohol consumption. Consumption of alcohol comes with a very great disadvantage – addiction. Thus those who cannot control their drinking, are better off without it and those who have never had a drink – stay away!!!

2. Age related and degenerative diseases have one and only one reason — a faulty lifestyle. Eating rich food, packaged food, fast food, excessively spicy food, more food, less food, smoking, alcohol abuse, late nights, work stress, strained interpersonal relationships, marital discord, emotional instability, too much of partying, can all lead to a one-way street where resides old friends such as hypertension, heart-related problems, diabetes, etc. Thus a balanced life is the most important criteria to enjoy a lifetime of good health and happiness.

3. A fibre rich diet increases your energy level. In a research conducted at Cardiff University, Wales, it was found that people who ate high-fibre cereals for breakfast they were more alert than others. According to the lead researcher Andrew Smith, Ph.D., fibre releases a fatty acid that the body uses for energy. Therefore, ensure to eat a fibre rich diet including whole wheat, brown bread, brown rice, bran flakes and our own very Indian ragi, jowar, bajra, etc.

4. Occasional fasting may actually be good for you in the long run. Research conducted at the National Institute of Ageing, USA, found that intermittent fasting produces better results than going on a strict calorie restricted diet. The reason, according to the study, the secret lies with the metabolic activity of the body. Eating every few hours keeps the blood sugar at high levels throughout. This sugar is ultimately metabolised to form energy. Oxidation is one of the by-products of this metabolic activity and these unstable oxygen molecules produced as a result causes wear and tear which lead to the degeneration of the system as a whole. But, remember, starving comes with a warning — skipping meals once too often may lead to some digestive problems, such as acidity and aggravation of peptic ulcers, if any. Further people on medication must consult their doctor before any change in their eating habits.

   In fact there is a diet known as 'eat every other day diet' which encourages obese and overweight people to avoid meals every other day. This is based on a research conducted by researchers in the National Institute on Ageing in Baltimore, where it was found that such a diet showed all the benefits of a calorie restricted diet. Besides causing the body to burn fat, it also triggers hormonal changes such as increasing the activity of two anti-ageing genes called SIRT3 and SIRT4. Analysis of a two-week trial revealed an impressive weight loss. In addition to blood pressure, heart rate and cholesterol were also lowered. But such a diet system need to be treated with caution as fasting is not advisable for those with health problems. Thus any such new ideas must be undertaken with the doctor's advice.

5. Sugar is the villain of the piece most of the time. Sugar as found in sweets, etc., are just not required for the body, especially after the age of forty. Fruits by themselves contain enough sugar to meet the body's needs. In fact even the consumption of fruits should be limited to limit the intake of calories. So reduce sugar in your tea, or better still cut it altogether and substitute it by adding a few drops of lemon.

6. There are almost 180 million people in the world today afflicted with diabetes., making it one of the most prevalent disease in the world. In fact this figure is set to double within the next twenty-five years, if drastic measures are not taken immediately. It is a real pity, because diabetes is a disease which attacks the organs and kills the person slowly and silently. That is why it is often called the 'silent killer'.

7. Vitamin E and C, when taken together may well protect the brain against the debilitating effects of Alzheimer's disease. In fact vitamin E and C are known to be anti-oxidants which slow-down the ageing process in the body. Researchers at the John Hopkins Bloomberg School of Public Health found that these two vitamins when taken together as supplements protect the elderly to reduce the effects of Alzheimer's disease. Needless to say any such doses have to be taken strictly under medical supervision.

8. That there is absolutely no need to count your calories. It is enough to have an idea of which food is rich in calories and avoid them. Soft drinks, pastries, sweets, chocolates, oil, butter, etc., are best reduced, if not avoided for a person whose BMI is in the overweight range. An obese person needs to crack down harder and ensure that the above food are kept at an arms length.

9. Men require around 2500 calories to maintain their weight, while women require about 2000 calories. See the chart and you will be amazed that one heavy meal – two servings chicken pulao / dal / raita gives you all the calories you need for the day!!! That's the reason why exercising is so important. Exercise burns the calories and enables us to lose weight without going on a starvation. See the chart in the next chapter for calories lost during exercise. But remember there is no need to count your calories. Just have a

rough idea of which food you can eat and which all you need to avoid.

10. Anti-oxidants have multiple benefits. A five-year study was published earlier this year in the Journal of the National Cancer Institute involving approximately 30,000 residents of North-Central China. They were given either a placebo or a dietary supplement of anti-oxidants. The participants who had the anti-oxidant supplement had a reduced cancer rate of 13 percent. In another study reported at the American Heart Association (AHA) Scientific Session, participants who consumed high amounts of antioxidant containing food had a 33 percent lower risk of heart attack and a 71 percent lower risk of stroke, than those who ate few antioxidant-containing food.

Note: Needless to say, if you have a heart problem or any other chronic disease, please refer to your doctor for the best advice. The above are generally for those without any major health problems.

FOOD FOR THOUGHT

Now let us look at a few specific food and their nutritional benefits for various parts of the body:

1. **Brain:** Carrots, broccoli, fish, fruits and vegetables are high in anti-oxidants.
2. **Eyes:** All food rich in vitamin C, E and lutein (citrus fruits).
3. **Lungs:** Food rich in beta carotene (mangoes, carrots, pumpkin, spinach).
4. **Heart:** Fruits, vegetables, grains, fat free and low-fat food, fish, lean meat and legumes.
5. **Bones:** Dairy products, dark green leafy vegetables, almonds, sunflower seeds.
6. **Skin:** Carotene rich food as mentioned.
7. **High:** Fibre food (oats, fruits, vegetables)
8. **Muscles and tissues:** Meats, pulses and other protein rich food.

CALORIE DENSITY

A new concept recently finding favour with dieticians is the calorie density. Diet surveys have revealed that low calorie density diet is better because you are then eating more vegetables, whole grains and less saturated fats.

Calorie density of any food is calculated by dividing its calories by its weight (in grams). It follows that if a food has fewer calories than grams, it has a calorie density less than 1.0. But while using the calorie density as a general guide, it should be remembered that there are other factors if food which also contribute to its quality such as vitamins, minerals, etc.

Following is the list of foods with their calorie density. It is not surprising that vegetables and fruits have the least calorie density and butter, oil, Mayonnaise, cheese, etc., have the maximum calorie density. One glance at this list will make you aware of which type of food to reduce and which to focus on.

Food	Calorie density
Cucumber	0.13
Tomato	0.21
Watermelon	0.32
Carrots	0.43
Orange	0.47
Apple	0.58
Paneer (cottage cheese)	0.73
Green Peas	0.78
Banana	0.92
Lentils (channa dal)	1.2
Rice	1.2
Pasta	1.4
Chicken Breast	1.7
Bread	2.6
Pizza	2.9
French Fries	3.2
Cheddar Cheese	4.1
Milk Chocolate Bar	5.4
Potato Chips	5.4
Peanuts	5.9
Butter	7.2
Mayonnaise	7.2
Salad or Cooking Oil	8.8

(Source: The volumetric Eating plan and U.S Dept of Agriculture)

Water, water everywhere

It has long been known that water is the healthiest of drinks for our body. Water flushes out the toxins from our body and keeps the system functioning efficiently. Our body cells are made up largely of water. A reduction of water level in the body can cause dehydration with drastic effects. Sufficient water is known to be good for the skin, organs, digestive system and various other every day problems.

It is not enough to drink water when we are thirsty. Being thirsty is an emergency signal from the body and we should learn to recognise the other signals much before that. In fact by drinking enough water you can ensure that your body remains hydrated all day long without having to give you any signals at all. A few simple points will ensure sufficient intake of water.

WATER THERAPY

Start the day by drinking at least two to three glasses of water. Some hydro therapists say that drinking 1.25 litres of water is the optimum amount to be consumed in the morning. But even two to three glasses of water taken first thing in the morning acts like a medicine. It gives the body the necessary hydration after a long night without any water, it helps to flush out the toxins built during the night and most importantly it ensures good bowel movement.

Make sure you drink at least one glass of water half an hour before every meal. This will ensure that your stomach is emptied and ready to absorb the nutrients you take in during the meal. Drink at least one glass of water half an hour after the meal to ensure enough hydration for the digestive process. If you are a tea or coffee drinker, drink a glass of water before every cup of tea or coffee.

If you are not the type to drink tea or coffee, remember to drink at least one glass of water in between meals. This will ensure that you have enough fluid intake during the day. In addition if you have been out sweating or exercising, be sure to drink a glass of water after a suitable period of 'cooling off' time.

There is no hard and fast rule as to how much water you must drink during the day. You have to learn to recognise the signals given by your body and ensure that you drink more than enough water.

In short, do not look for any magic formulas as to how much to drink and when to drink. Just ensure that you drink enough water early in the morning on an empty stomach, that you drink water half an hour before, after and in between every meal, that you drink sufficient water after any hectic activity and finally sign off the day with a glass of water. This will ensure sufficient hydration required for the body to function normally.

Fitness experts suggest that a person exercising should drink about 200– 400 ml of water before starting to exercise. In addition, during the exercise, drink about 200–250 ml for every 20 minutes of exercise. Finally drink about 400-800 ml of water after the exercise is over (for every pound of weight loss).

Points to ponder :

1. Calculate your Body Mass Index (BMI). It will help you to control your weight better when you know that you are slipping into the 'clinically obese' category. But action must be initiated as soon as the overweight category is reached.

2. Obesity can be due to various factors : from childhood due to overindulgent parents, due to physiological problems or due to bad eating habits coupled with inactivity. Although some of these factors cannot be avoided altogether, a bit of retrospection and discipline will go a long way in controlling obesity.

3. Whatever the reason, a bit of tweaking of your lifestyle, in most cases, is sufficient to bring your weight under control to have a better and a healthier life. But clinically obese people require urgent medical intervention if they are to avoid organ damage. The stakes are too high and all efforts must be made to control the weight.

4. Obesity is usually due to an excess of calorie intake as compared to consumption. The body is genetically conditioned to convert excess calories into fat stored by the body in various parts (usually around the abdomen, hips and thighs) to be used at a later stage when food may be scarce. But some obese people do continue to remain obese in spite of controlling their diet and reducing the intake of calories. Such people require urgent medical attention.

5. Thus one of the surest means of controlling obesity is by limiting the intake of calories and burning these calories through exercise and activity. Starvation is not the solution since it deprives the body of valuable nutrients. Although some positive results may be observed during a starvation diet, the ill-effects of the subsequent lack of vitamins and nutrients can be quite serious. Hence, moderation of eating habits is required and not starvation.

6. The correct way to go about it is to be aware of the different food groups and change your eating habits ever so slightly that you reduce calorie intake, while ensuring a balanced diet. Take informed decisions regarding your eating habits and you will find your body responding favourably. Educate yourself about the different food groups and the ill-effects of overeating, snacking, eating junk food, etc., and soon enough the urge will come from within you to avoid such food altogether.

7. Don't fall for gimmicks and hard sell tactics by savvy companies. All you need is a sensible diet which is balanced, and at the same time reduces your total calorie consumption. All the various diets,

meal replacements programmes, magic potions, etc., are more harmful than useful to your long-term health. If you cannot exert the necessary will power to control your diet, it is better to remain obese than fall prey to one of these programmes which can actually harm you.

8. Avoid rich and oily food. Go for more vegetables and fibre rich food. Avoid junk and packaged food, eat in moderation and educate yourself about what you are eating. Lead an active life with enough exercise to keep you fit. This in essence is the magic potion to a happy and a long life.

"The wise are instructed by reason; ordinary minds by experience; the stupid, by necessity; and brutes by instinct"

– Cicero

***

4

FITNESS MANAGEMENT

> *"Lack of activity destroys the good condition of every human being, while movement and methodical physical exercise save it and preserve it."*
>
> *– Plato*

Fitness is one of the most important aspects of our life. As long as one is fit and healthy he can face all the challenges that life hurls at him. Although it does not require too much of effort to remain fit and healthy, some amount of discipline and an inner urge is required to lead a balanced life, which is the most important requirement for fitness.

Everybody knows what happens to a machine when it is left unused and unattended for long. It gets rusted, the parts get seized up and the machine stops working. The same fate awaits a vehicle which is left unused for long. Thus all machines need to be used regularly in order to ensure proper functioning.

Our body is like a machine. It requires care and constant use. If we do not exercise, our muscles and joints become atrophied and their function slows down. Thus exercise is of prime importance for the proper functioning of our body.

Exercise has many other benefits. It is good for the heart. Exercise improves blood circulation and the heart has to work harder. The heart is also a muscle. So any form of exercise can be said to be a cardiovascular exercise which improves the blood circulation and pumps more blood into the heart.

The question is - what exactly are cardiovascular exercises ? Simply said, any exercise involving large muscle groups in a continuous activity can be termed as a cardiovascular exercise. Such activities create higher demand for oxygen and makes the heart pump harder to supply blood that carries oxygen to the cells and tissues. Thus, walking, jogging, running, swimming, climbing, etc., can all be termed as cardiovascular activities.

All forms of exercise makes you breathe hard as more oxygen is required. Thus it makes your lungs work more efficiently. In other words, exercise is also good for the lungs.

EXERCISE AND CALORIES

Exercise burns calories. Most of us eat more than required. If our body needs about 2000 calories, we eat more than 2500 calories every day. So where do these extra calories go? Imagine your body to be a tub. You are putting in 2500 units every day, but removing only 2000 units. So, what happens to the balance 500 units ? It remains in the tub. Similarly the balance calories are converted to fat by the body and stored for the rainy day. And where does the body store this excess fat ? Mainly around the waist, hips and thighs. That's the reason why the first sign of putting on weight is an increasing waistline.

Now imagine that before your body can convert and store these excess calories you are able to utilise them. What happens? Now that there are no excess calories, the body cannot convert them to fat, hence you stop putting on weight. And how do you get rid of these excess calories ? By exercising, be it walking, jogging, swimming or playing outdoor games. By exercising you are in fact increasing the metabolic rate of your body and converting these calories into energy. Muscles burn more calories, so a muscular person has a lesser tendency to put on weight. Thus a person who is exercising is not only burning calories during exercise, but the muscles developed during exercise also burn more calories round the clock. In the process, you become fit, trim and healthy. In addition, you keep all sorts of illnesses at bay and delay the ageing process of your body.

Exercise as a muscle toner and stress buster

Another advantage of exercise is that it tones your muscles leaving you looking and feeling trim and fit. By doing some abdominal exercises the musculature around your abdomen will become stronger. Coupled with the fact that you are on a sensible diet (thus ingesting only what is enough for you) and you are losing the excess calories, you will find that not only will your weight be under control, but also that your wayward tummy will also be reined in and you will be a much healthier individual all-round.

It has been clinically proven that exercise is a stress buster. When you exercise, certain chemicals are released into the blood stream which relaxes the system and serves to ease the tension within. In today's harried world when everyone is stressed and worried, a daily dose of exercise is a great way to relax and take your mind off the nitty gritties and focus on something entirely different such as your workout.

Exercise is also good for the organs. Be it the kidneys, liver, lungs, all parts of the body benefit from exercise in many ways.

Advantages of regular exercise

Therefore, the advantages of exercise are as follows:

1. It is restorative for the heart.
2. It is good for the lungs.
3. It helps you to burn off extra calories and thereby control your weight.
4. It tones your muscles, leaving you with a trimmer physique.
5. It relaxes your body and is a great stress buster.
6. It slows down the ageing process of the body.
7. It prevents or reduces depression even when you are going through bad times.
8. It makes you feel energetic and confident of yourself.
9. It improves your posture and walking style.

Now that we have agreed that exercise is good for health and further that every health-conscious person must get some form of exercise or the other, let us explore the various types of exercises that you can do. Each individual must find his or her own level and adopt an exercise regimen best suited according to their likes, dislikes and lifestyle.

DIFFERENT TYPES OF EVERYDAY EXERCISES

There are various common types of exercises that can be adopted.

1. Walking
2. Running
3. Swimming
4. Free-style exercises
5. Yoga
6. Gym workouts
7. Aerobics
8. Outdoor games

We will now define each of the above in order to help you to find which combination of these you can follow with optimum results. Depending on which activity is most suitable for you, considering your lifestyle and the amount of time you can dedicate, you can select one or more of the activities. But remember dedication is the catchword and you have to put in the requisite effort if you want to see tangible results.

The aim of every exercise regime is to burn calories, improve blood circulation and muscle toning and improve cardiovascular functions. Anita Bean, author of The Complete Guide to Sports Nutrition (A & C Black) has spelt out very clearly that exercising on an empty stomach will only result in a sluggish metabolism, less muscle tone and poorer fitness. For best results it is advisable to exercise two to four hours after a meal. And a meal within two hours of the exercise would be just right to lose glycogen and boost the metabolic rate which is necessary for a weight loss.

But I would perhaps add a rider to the above — a morning walk is a great exercise, metabolism or no metabolism!

WALKING FOR HEALTH

Walking is one of the best exercises for all seasons. Not only is brisk walking an excellent cardiovascular exercise, it also burns off those extra calories and helps you to relax and concentrate your mind. There is nothing like an early morning walk when the pollution levels are low and the mad rush has not yet started. Haul yourself out of that comfortable bed and onto the streets. Get a lungful of cool fresh air and feel the difference. Watch the city wake up slowly and get down to business.

Once you are in the habit of morning walk, it becomes addictive and your day will never be the same again unless you have had the walk. Walking is a great form of exercise, because regardless of age everyone can walk, young or old, weak or strong.

People who walk regularly are proved to be healthier and age slower than sedentary people. In fact walking is said to be an anti-depressant as well. Those who are used to a morning or an evening walk will swear by it and in fact look forward to the time when they can hit the streets. So get on with it!!

Walking is easy and convenient

Walking requires no training, no fees, no courses, no special clothes or shoes. All it requires is that you should be on the road or in the park. In fact walking is one exercise that you can do even when you are not feeling fully fit. On those days when you are feeling under, you can go for a stroll and the days when you feel on top of the world, you can really ramp up your walking speed. Walking is a highly flexible mode of exercise.

So, put on those jeans, T-shirt, sneakers or whatever you have, get out in the open and get started. You will never regret this habit for as long as you live and that would be a lot longer than non-walkers. On rainy days you can even walk around in your house to get all the benefits of walking.

How much to walk? What speed to walk at? There are so many questions.

Not to worry. Take a brisk walk for at least half an hour daily to achieve the minimum results. If you have time off from your busy schedule and can spare an hour for your walk, all the better. Remember strolling is no good. The walk should be brisk enough to make you breathe hard and to make your heart beat faster. If you are one of those who go for a morning walk swith your friends, chatting along the way, then forget it and stay at home. Don't bother about going for a walk, for this is not going to do much good to you. Remember, the trick is to walk briskly. The faster you walk, the better it is. In fact it is a good technique to walk as fast as you can for about five minutes, then slow down your speed and walk a bit slower for the next five minutes. Then again start off briskly. This way you will not feel tired, but at the same time it will keep your heart pumping hard throughout the period.

An evening walk if not a morning walk!

If you do not have time for a morning walk due to your job schedule, you can instead go for an evening walk. But evening walks are best taken on roads with less traffic, to avoid inhaling the fumes of the vehicles. Select a route for yourself that avoids the busy roads, and stick to the quiet by lanes, where you can walk in peace without the honking and screeching of impatient vehicles. In fact many people find that an evening walk after a hard day's work at the office, helps them to unwind and get rid of the unwanted stresses. An early morning walk may be a trifle tiresome for people who have a hard day ahead of them and would want to arrive fresh at the office. For them an evening walk is a good solution.

RUNNING / JOGGING

For those of you who are younger, a good run is much better than a walk. Running is a better cardiovascular exercise and you obviously burn more calories when you run rather than walk. But people who are over forty must be cautious and consult their doctor before they start running. Thus for these people walking is a much safer bet than running. But if you are healthy and your doctor has checked you and given you the green signal, then running or jogging is a better option any day.

In fact a study conducted by a Stanford University produced evidence that people in the older age group who run regularly live longer and have fewer age-related problems. Further they were less likely to have problems performing day to day tasks such as eating, walking, etc. But remember, for a person who has been inactive all his life, it is better to take it easy and go for brisk walks rather than start running or jogging straightaway.

And for people who are not young, it is always better to discuss with your doctor before embarking on an ambitious exercise regimen.

Jogging is in fact one of the best cardiovascular exercises burning around 130 calories in 10 minutes. It uses almost all the major muscle groups in the body and also reduces the risk of heart disease, diabetes and hypertension.

When you begin to run it is always advisable to start with a walk that warms up the muscles. Even car manufacturers warn drivers against zipping up straight-away on a cold engine. First you have to warm the engine, then slowly proceed from one gear to the next before hitting the road. Similarly when you set out for a run, you have to first warm up by walking normally, then briskly before starting to run. Similarly running should be ended with a walk to cool down.

Run a little, jog a little

It is enough to jog for no more than half an hour every day for beginners. This will ensure that you do not put on weight and start the slow slide back. As you get used to the running schedule, this time can be increased slowly to a maximum of one hour. Very often we try to put in too much effort initially and find that we are unable to cope. Thus it is better to start slowly and build up as the stamina improves.

People over forty should not run continuously for a long period. It is a good idea to jog lightly for a short distance and then walk for some time before breaking into a jog again. This way you ensure that you do not tax your system more than necessary. And always, please listen to what your body is telling you. If you feel tired or breathless, discontinue immediately or slow down the tempo. Consult a doctor if you are in the least doubt.

Finally there is no need to run as if you are practicing for the Olympics. Depending on your age, physical shape, stamina, etc., running can be anything from a slow and comfortable jog to a fast canter. People who are out of shape will do well to start with walking and slowly upgrade to jogging and running as they get in shape and build up their stamina.

So get started ! Start with a slow walk, build up to a brisk walk and then break into a jog. Do this at least six times a week and you will feel a positive difference within a few days. You will notice your pulse rate drop as your stamina builds, a sign that your heart is getting stronger. You will feel less tired and more energetic throughout the day and sleep better during the night.

Remember, if you have a health problem or find any unusual aches and pains or niggles, you need to consult a doctor before proceeding with your activity. First timers often end up with cramps and strains and need to take it easy for the first few days. Ignoring a problem can lead to more serious complications. Thus no matter which activity you are taking up, listen to your body's signals and if you are in any doubt consult a doctor before proceeding any further. The idea is to get the maximum benefit without torturing your body.

SWIMMING

Swimming is undoubtedly one of the best exercises. Whether it be burning calories, muscle toning, cardiovascular benefits or stress reduction, swimming for half an hour every day is as good as it gets.

Unfortunately, many of us do not have access to a swimming pool. Most swimming pools are within exclusive clubs for the use of club members only. Then there are many swimming clubs which open their gates to the public, for a price. But the timing of these swimming clubs may not suit office goers. Again due to the demand for swimming and the commercial nature of the swimming clubs, there will invariably be overcrowding in such pools, leaving the serious swimmer frustrated.

Going to a swimming pool involves traveling to and from the pool, time for change of rig, etc. All this demands an adequate amount of spare time, which in today's hectic world is difficult to find. Practically, most working people would not be able to take up swimming regularly. In fact even swimming for an hour twice a week is known to be good for the body. You don't have to go swimming everyday, just twice a week is also enough.

Although swimming is a wonderful exercise, most of us have to get by without this luxury. But, relax, you are not missing much. If you do have access to a swimming pool, then great, go ahead and dive right in, if not, no problems, there are many other forms of exercise which will give you the same result.

FREE-STYLE EXERCISES

If there were marks to be awarded to the mentioned group of exercises, then free-style exercises would undoubtedly get the highest marks.

Free-style exercises provide all the benefits which you get from all other forms of exercises. There are many forms of free-style cardiovascular exercises, which exercise different muscle groups. Free-style exercises provide the maximum muscle toning, since you can exercise specific group of muscles, and you can burn all the calories you want through free-style exercises.

You can do free-style exercises in the privacy of your bedroom and in whatever outfit you care to wear. There are plenty of free-style exercises out there, catering to every requirement. I diligently go through the following workouts for about 30 minutes every day and it suits me just fine.

These free-style exercises have multiple benefits. Your workout can include all of them or you can stagger them – do some one day and the others the next day.

1. **Arm stretches:** Stand with your feet about two feet apart. Lift your arms forward in front of you, palms together. Next, spread your arms sideways in level with your shoulders taking a deep breath while you do so. Then bring back the palms in clapping position forward again. Do this about twenty to thirty times. This exercise will increase your lung power and strengthen your shoulders.

2. **Alternate hand stretches:** Stand with your feet about two feet apart and lift your right hand straight up till it points to the sky. Now, bring the right hand down while taking the left hand up. At the extreme your hands should be 180 degrees apart. You must feel your waist stretching on the side of your hand which is pointing up. Do this about twenty to thirty times. This exercise tones the muscles on either side of your abdomen. This will help rein in those 'love handles' or 'tyres of fat' on either side.

3. **Side stretches:** Stand with your feet about two feet apart, lift the right hand up and bend your body to the left side, bringing the right hand over your head and down on the other side. Remain in this position for about five seconds, trying to slide your left hand down your leg as far as possible. Now straighten up and repeat the same with the right side. Once again you must feel your sides stretching. Do this about twenty to thirty times.

4. **Twist jumps:** While jumping up and down on your toes twist you torso to either side. Do this fast for about fifty to sixty times. This exercise has two functions. One to pump up your heart beat and second to strengthen the muscles on your torso. Remember you have to twist you body hard to get the maximum benefit. But don't overdo it as you may end up with a sprained back.

5. **Trunk twisting:** Standing with your feet about two feet apart, twist your body from side to side, keeping your hands on your waist. Do this for about twenty to thirty times either side. This exercise will achieve same as (2) above as well as your torso muscles.

6. **Shoulder exercise:** Keep your fingers on your shoulder bone, with arms bent at the elbow. Your arms must be straight out. Now, lift your arm all the way, i.e., swing up as far as it can go, taking a deep breath as you do so and bring down all the way. Do this up and down for twenty to thirty times. This will give you stronger shoulder muscles and prevent shoulder dislocations, etc., in old age.

7. **Neck turns:** Stand with your feet about two feet apart. Roll your head from one side to the other, keeping your head bent forward, i.e., trying to touch your chest with your chin. Now roll back to the other side, but with your head thrown back all the way. When this is done continuously it will be like your head going in a circle. To avoid dizziness, do this ten times on one side and ten times on the other. You can then repeat the cycle again.

8. **Dynamic neck push:** Stand straight with your feet apart. Clasp your hands behind your head and push the head against your hands. This will develop your neck muscles. Coupled with the neck turns, these two exercises will help to keep spondilytis at bay.

9. **Toe–touching:** Those of you without any known back problems can now do some forward bending toe-touching exercises, taking care not to bend your knees. Do this about twenty times with both hands together, and another twenty times alternate toe-touching i.e., while the right fingers are touching the left toe, the left hand is all the way up, pointing to the sky. This exercise will give you overall flexibility while toning your abdominal muscles.

   Note : People with back pain should generally avoid any sort of forward bending.

10. **Back bends:** Stand with your feet apart, hands on your waist, thumb in front, palm at the back, fingers pointing down, clench your buttock muscles and slowly bend backwards as far as you can go. Remain at the maximum position to the count of five, then straighten up and relax your buttock muscles. Repeat this exercise ten times. This exercise will tone your abdominal muscles and strengthen the muscles of your back and buttocks. Especially good for people with low back pain and other back problems caused basically due to weak back muscles.

11. **Wall stretches:** Stand facing a wall with your chest touching the wall. Lift your arms straight up and touch the wall with the tips of your fingers. Now 'walk' up and down the wall with your finger tips. While in this position, clench and release the muscles with which you control the flow of urine. Do this twenty times and then step back 'walking' down the wall with your finger tips. Repeat the whole process once more. This exercise stretches your body, improves the posture and tones the muscles.

12. **Sit-ups:** Stand with you feet apart, raise your arms horizontally in front of you, and lower yourself to a sitting position. Now haul yourself up briskly. Remember, you must go all the way down before coming up again. This exercise is good for the hip and thigh muscles and thus is excellent for ladies who tend to put on weight

around their hips and thighs. Do sit-ups for about twenty to thirty times, take one minute jogging break and repeat again.

13. **Push-ups:** Do ten push-ups on your palms, keeping your body straight all the time. Next, repeat the same on your fingertips. You can also try on your knuckles for variety. Initially do a total of thirty push-ups building up slowly to sixty as your stamina builds up. This exercise is wonderful for your biceps, triceps, quadriceps, forearms, wrists, fingers and other body parts. Naturally ladies do not need bulging biceps, hence can just do a total of five to ten push-ups for muscle toning. Ladies can substitute this by sit-ups.

14. **Crunches:** Lie on your back, adjacent to a low bed or chair. Put your feet up on the bed such that your leg is bent at right angles at the knees and as close as possible to the bed. Now clasp your hands behind your head and lift yourself as much as possible. Repeat this for about twenty to thirty times. You will feel a pulling sensation in you stomach. That is your abdominal muscles objecting at having to work suddenly. As days pass you will notice the sensation reducing. Once you finish the first cycle of crunches, switch to one round of diagonal crunches, then repeat the whole cycle once more. Those with back problems can skip the crunches and go straight to the diagonal crunches. Crunches are good for building up the abdominal muscles.

15. **Diagonal crunches:** Lie as above, but instead of going straight up, try to touch your left knee with the right elbow and vice versa. Do this for twenty to thirty times for two cycles. Diagonal crunches not only builds up the abdominal muscles, but also tone the muscles on the sides of the waist, thereby reducing the 'tyres'.

16. **Leg lifts:** Lie flat on your back and raise your feet six inches above the ground. Keep your leg straight and hold this position to a slow count of twenty. Lower your feet slowly. Repeat the same exercise ten to twenty times. This exercise strengthens the abdominal and hip muscles.

17. **Alternate trunk twists:** Lie flat on your back. Bend your knees and fold your legs. Now try to touch the left ankle with the right knee and vice versa. Do this twenty to thirty times. This exercise strengthens the back muscles as well as tones the abdominal muscles. Generally you should feel a burning pain in the pit of your stomach. This means that your abdominal muscles are being exercised.

18. **Bhujangasan:** Lie on your stomach with your palms flat on the floor by the side of your face. Now lift your torso by arching, without taking much weight on your hands. Do this twenty to thirty times. This exercise is a stress buster and strengthens the shoulder and chest muscles.

19. **Lie on stomach leg lift:** Lie as above with your hands by the side. Now lift one leg about twelve inches off the floor and cross the leg over the other le.g. Hold this position for a slow count of twenty. Now repeat with the other le.g. Repeat the cycle once more. This exercise is good for toning the abdominal muscles.

20. **Side crunches:** Lie straight on your side. Try to lift your left shoulder up and reach out for your ankle with your right hand. Hold at the maximum stretch for a few seconds and come back to the normal position. Repeat ten times. Now turn to the other side and repeat another ten times. This will take some of the flab off your waist and tone your abdominal muscles.

21. **Shavasan:** Lie on your back in the classical prone position. Relax all your muscles. Focus on each part of the body and relax that part, such as feet, calves, knees, thighs, etc., all the way till your head. Once this is over lie absolutely still for a couple of minutes.

The type, variety, time period and intensity of the exercise that you can do are not limited to the above. You can do any sort of activity for any period provided your body takes it. The most important point to remember is to listen to your body every time, so that you do not unnecessarily tax your body and end up with cramps, sprains, etc. If you are doing any sort of intense exercise or activity such as, training with weights, long distance running, etc., please be sure to consult a doctor or take professional help from a trainer before you start any such activity.

A sample workout for good health

If you can set aside 45 minutes each day for an exercise regime, good health, satisfaction and a fitter and trimmer body will be the benefits you can reap.

Before we start, let us see what is the best time for doing this is. My answer is any time that is suitable keeping in mind your activities for the day. It is a good idea to workout in the evening in the privacy of your room. As morning is the better time for a walk or a run, evening can be reserved for the workout. Of course you need not be fanatical about the workout and cancel all your evening programmes. You can mix and match your routine so that you get to do this workout at least five times a week. Even office-goers and others who are busy throughout the day will feel relieved and relaxed after the workout. It is not even necessary that you have to go for a morning walk or a jog; it all depends on your daily schedule.

So decide when you can spare the time and the energy for it. Some studies have found that exercising two to three hours after a meal burns more calories than at other times. But the difference is not too much. Rather than geting bogged down by what time is suitable for this, decide on a time which is suitable for you and which you can sustain. But generally avoid any sort of exercise or other physical activity immediately after a full meal.

Walking

Start with a brisk walk. You need not look for a park or a wide road. Even your home is good enough for a brisk walk, as long as there is enough place to manoeuvre without knocking down the furniture. The walk should be fast enough for you to start panting slightly. You can intersperse the walk every few minutes with a burst of hectic activity such as running, on-the-spot jogging, etc. The idea is to make your heart beat faster, increase your blood flow and respiration, thus making more oxygen available to the tissues and muscles for metabolism.

Do this for at least fifteen minutes, if not more.

Free-style exercises

After every four or five groups of exercises you must jog for five minutes. If you cannot jog, a brisk walk is a good substitute. Again, the idea is to keep the heart pumping hard throughout the exercise period. You can even skip for hundred counts once in a while. Even if you do not have a skipping rope you can do 'simulation skipping' i.e., close your eyes, imagine you have a skipping rope in your hands and skip. The effect is the same if you do it diligently.

The whole workout should take about 45 minutes to one hour. Try this and you will see a definite improvement in your health within 30 days. You will feel fitter and more energetic. Slowly your weight will also start decreasing. Of course this has to be complemented with sensible eating habits.

MONITOR YOUR PULSE

Keep a check on your pulse rate. According to medical experts, the maximum pulse rate during workout should not exceed the maximum permissible as mentioned. Calculate the following: Subtract your age from 200. Your heart beat must be above 60% of the figure you get and below 80% of the same figure. In other words, if you are forty years old, then your heart beat should be between 96 and 128 while you exercise. Initially you may find your pulse rate nearing this figure and you may even have to go easy so as not to exceed this figure. But as the days go by and you build up your stamina you will find that you can comfortably keep exercising without coming too close to the maximum pulse rate.

Similarly, you will find your normal pulse rate also going down as days go by. All this is because your heart is also a muscle. By making it work hard you are developing it and thus it has to beat slower to deliver the required amount of blood. In other words, the efficiency of the heart increases and therefore the pulse rate decreases.

What I have described above are simple every day exercises that everybody can do. There is no need for expensive gyms, trainers, physiotherapists, gadgets, etc., and of course it costs nothing except your time and will power.

Many of you would probably be able to afford to go to fancy gyms but there are also a whole lot of exercise gadgets and places available which may actually be good for you. There are aerobics centres where some people get together and do aerobics under the watchful eyes of a trained instructor. Then there are multi-gyms with plenty of fancy equipments and expert trainers who will take you step by step, through the workout.

TONE THROUGH GYROTONICS

Then there is the latest fad called gyrotonics which is a form of physical alignment and deep muscle control. Gyrotonics basically consisits of about fifty exercises, with more than a hundred variations which involve bending, twisting, stretching and turning the muscles and the skeletal system. Needless to say it involves the latest and most expensive machinery and is offered at selected health centres, obviously for an exorbitant fee. All workouts and training in gyms have to be done under a trainer so as not to overstress the body.

If you do not have the resources to afford the above fancy stuff, not to worry. There is no doubt that places like multi-gyms and gyrotonic centres are good for you, but the good old exercise regime which I have mentioned is as good if not better. And you can do them anytime, anywhere, alone or with someone. They do not need trainers because they are not harmful if done without assistance. They do not need fancy equipment. For the exercises mentioned, you need not spend a fortune on your track suits or training shoes. Just an old pair of jeans and sneakers would do as well.

The best part is that there is no evidence to suggest that any of the above hi-tech training programmes are in any way superior to the simple exercise regime mentioned here. The results you will get in your overall health including weight reduction and cardiovascular benefits, by following the everyday pattern of simple exercises are as good, if not better, than the other forms of training.

But as I have said before, there is no magic potion, no weight reducing tablets, no fat dissolvers, no gastric bypass, no trainer overseeing your activities, no nutritionist counting your calories and no equipment to train on. And that's why it is healthy and involves no side effects. But a lot of will power and inner resolve is required to start, continue and maintain the exercise regime along with healthy eating habits mentioned earlier.

Note :

1. The above workout mainly exercises the muscles of the abdomen, back, hips, thighs, shoulders and arms. At the same time they tone other muscles.
2. Those of you with back pain (or any other affliction) should obviously consult your doctor before embarking on any exercise regime. People with back pain are often advised not to bend forward and so such exercises may not be suitable for them.
3. In fact those with problems such as hypertension, thyroid, heart problems, etc., should get a general clearance from their doctors before embarking on any sort of an exercise regime.
4. I am sure that many of you who have read ads or other propaganda about reducing weight by exercising just twenty minutes a day for three days a week will be disappointed after seeing the exercises mentioned here which have to be done every day. If you believe that exercising for twenty minutes a day for three days a week is going to make a difference, then you must also believe that the moon is made of cheese. It just doesn't work that way. You have to work hard if you need to see results. Remember nothing is for free. There are no free lunches in the big bad world. If you want something, you've got to work for it. So be prepared to spend those forty minutes to one hour at least six days a week if you need to see yourself reducing. In fact for better results you may well add another half an hour of brisk walking or jogging at least three times a week.
5. The trick is to keep your heart pumping continuously for these forty minutes. So, for the initial couple of weeks, have a watch ready to monitor your pulse from time to time. Thus you can increase or decrease your effort so that you are within the limits, as mentioned above. Once you have got the hang of it, you do not need the watch any more.
6. Those who have the capacity for more can complement this by skipping for about five hundred times. Remember the trimmer you want to be, the harder you have to work. But the exercises described above are by themselves enough. Walking, jogging, running, swimming, skipping, etc., help to burn those extra calories and are additionally good cardiovascular exercises.
7. Avoid wearing high heels. Try to wear soft soled flats instead. This will ensure that you do not damage your back. People who spend

a lifetime wearing high heeled shoes invariably spend their old age suffering from chronic back pain. This is because high heels tip the pelvis forward and alter the delicate balance in the spine.

8. Never cradle the phone between your ear and shoulder. In today's age of mobile telephones, it is a common sight to see people walking about with their mobile phone wedged between their ear and shoulder. While this is a great way of keeping your hands free permitting you to continue working, it is better to invest in a hands-free phone or use the headset which is available with every phone. Otherwise you may end up with spondilytis, which can affect you for the rest of your life.

So, get set, put on your dancing shoes and get started !!!

SMOKING

Bad news for all you smokers. Studies have proved beyond doubt that smoking is the single most important factor that can lead to ill-health. Cigarette smoke has many dangerous elements, many of them carcinogens which can wreck you beyond recovery. Most smokers are immune to any advice to quit smoking, mainly because they are bombarded day in and day out with such advices. Right from the Surgeon General's warning to the numerous articles in various newspapers and magazines, the chant is '*Smoking is dangerous, smoking will destroy your health, quit smoking immediately ....*' The fact that smokers continue to smoke in spite of all dire warnings indicate that either they do not believe all that is said against smoking, or that the pleasure they get from smoking far outweighs any possible ill-effects.

Why do I repeat the same advice that you have been getting ever since you started smoking ? Because, the fact that you are reading this book indicates that you are concerned about your health.

Keep smoking

So my advice to you is 'don't stop smoking!!' I know that smoking gives you pleasure, smoking eases the tension building within you during stressful times, smoking gives you that macho feeling and last, but not the least, smoking is addictive. If you are a regular smoker, your body probably needs the nicotine to function smoothly. So, 'don't stop smoking', because I know that if I say – 'stop smoking', it's going to fall on deaf ears. I know that smokers will continue to read this book, pretending that this section does not exist.

Reduce the number

So, all my dear smokers, don't stop smoking. For even if you do stop smoking for the time being, sooner or later the urge to smoke will overcome your will power and you will take up smoking again with a vengeance. So don't stop smoking, but reduce the number of cigarettes you smoke. Every cigarette less that you smoke in a day will lessen the ill-effects. Remember, cigarette smoke is a silent and slow killer. The more cigarettes you smoke, the more toxins will get into your blood and the more ill-effects you will have later on in life. Conversely, the less you smoke, lesser amounts of toxins will be absorbed into your system. More important, by reducing the number of cigarettes you smoke in a day, you are giving an important message to your system that your will power is the boss. Once your system gets this message, it will be easier for you to smoke lesser cigarettes until finally one day you have overcome this addiction and thus opened yet another window towards better health.

Remember, the trick is not to aim for the sky. I have heard many people saying that if you need to stop smoking, you have to stop completely. I do not agree with this theory. For a regular smoker, a smoke is a necessity and by stopping completely one fine day, chances are that you will revert to smoking the next day. If you are a chain smoker, start reducing slowly, month by month. Once you have made up your mind that you wish to stop smoking, give yourself a time limit, say three months during which you can taper off your smoking. Start by smoking only after meals, or tea, or at times when you feel stressed. Stop smoking out of habit and boredom. When you have nothing to do, don't reach for that cigarette. Instead go for a brisk walk. The most dangerous habit is smoking out of boredom. Kill that habit and your battle is half won.

Finally, stop smoking altogether

As you get used to smoking at specific intervals, cut down a little more. Do this gradually until you are down to three or four cigarettes a day. Once you reach this point, you have practically won the battle. The next step for you is to stop carrying cigarettes and look for one when you do need it. Once you have stopped smoking and your body has lost the urge to smoke, you will feel healthier and more energetic.

The fact is that smoking is injurious for your long-term health. Heart problems, diabetes, hypertension, all these and more may get exacerbated by smoking. Further the possibility of lung cancer always hangs above a smokers' head like Damocles' sword. Add to that the fact that with so many toxins finding their way to the blood stream and hence to the tissues, tissue regeneration is seriously hampered leading to acceleration in the ageing process.

Then come the indirect effects which are as serious, if not worse. It has long been known that in the long run passive smoking is as bad as smoking. Spouses of heavy smokers have reported symptoms which are generally associated with the smokers themselves. Passive smoking is extremely dangerous for children, whose immature respiratory system simply cannot cope with the smoke and soon develop serious respiratory problems.

Smoking also leads to blindness in older people. Researchers at the University of California, Los Angeles found that smokers had 11% higher rates of age-related macular degeneration (AMD) – which causes loss of vision, than non-smokers of the same age.

It has been long proved that smoking constitutes real danger for pregnant women, leading to complications in delivery, damage to the foetus and worse. Even passive smoking is dangerous at this delicate stage.

POINTS TO PONDER :

1. An exercise regime coupled with good eating habits and a moderate lifestyle is the one and only way for good health.
2. Exercise is the single solution for all your problems. It burns your excess calories, it is good for your heart and general health, it is a stress buster and drives away your blues.
3. Walking, running, swimming and free-style exercises are some of the most common and helpful ways to better health.
4. Fourty-five minutes of good free-style exercise, coupled with a walking or running programme are enough to guarantee long- term health.
5. Exercise is a great way to remain young, mentally and physically. Certain hormones released during exercise fight ageing of the cells. It is a known fact that people who exercise are less prone to Alzheimers', disease and other problems associated with old age, such as arthritis, etc.
6. If you are a smoker, remember that ill-health is knocking at your door. It not only harms your health, but also the health of your near and dear ones. In addition, it drains your pocket, one which you can do without. So, kick the habit now and live a healthier life.
7. Avoid the many fancy clinics coming up all over the place like mushrooms after a rain. No doubt, some of them offer results that flatter. It is a fact that some of these clinics promise, and really deliver weight loss of over 15 kgs in a short period of time. But this sort of weight loss is at best temporary, because the moment the treatment is stopped, the weight shows a marked increase.
8. Weight lost the natural way, through a balanced diet, exercise and a healthy life rarely comes back. In addition the habits that you pick up during this effort ensure that you avoid debilitating age-related diseases.
9. Exercise is a stress buster, and is good for the heart. Hormones released during exercise helps the body to fight stress. By exercising

we are taking our mind off any immediate problems that we may be facing, hence exercise is a good remedy for depression.

10. Due to increased cardiovascular activity and subsequent blood circulation, exercise is a skin toner. People who exercise regularly have a better skin than their sedentary counterparts. This increased blood circulation not only helps the skin but the organs, as well as each and every part of the body by bringing more oxygen rich blood and removing the toxics more effectively.
11. Finally, it is exercise all the way. With so many advantages it's a wonder why people are so reluctant to spend an extra hour at it. Whether to lose weight, to remain young, to keep away illnesses or simply to have a good physique, exercise comes the winner in every department. And the best part— its side effects are also advantageous.

Type of Exercises	Calories/hour
Sleeping	55
Eating	85
Sitting	85
Standing	100
Driving	110
Office work	140
Housework, moderate	160+
Walking, 3mph	280
Table Tennis	290
Tennis	350+
Aerobics	450+
Bicycling, moderate	450+
Jogging, 5mph	500
Swimming, active	500+
Rowing	550+
Squash	650+
Skipping with rope	700+
Running	700+

***

5

STRESS MANAGEMENT

> *"There is more to life than increasing its speed."*
> *– Mohandas K. Gandhi*

This topic has been in the limelight of late for a very valid reason. The pace of life and living has been increasing steadily during the last two decades and the stress levels are proportionately increasing. Today, almost 600 million people worldwide are estimated to be suffering from hypertension.

Let us begin by defining 'stress'. Clinically, stress is an adaptive response of the body to a potentially threatening event. In such a situation, the body prepares itself for what is termed as the 'fight or flight' response. This simply means that the body is ready to fight and face the situation or take flight. To facilitate this, the heart beats faster in order to pump more blood throughout the body. Thus the blood pressure and the pulse increases.

STRESS AS AN ADAPTIVE RESPONSE OF THE BODY

In ancient times, primitive people had to face life threatening situations every minute of their lives. To survive they had to either fight and overcome the threat or run for their lives and escape. Both situations for quick response called from the mind and body which is possible by pumping more blood into the brain and the body resulting in the heart responding by pumping harder. Thus stress was basically an adaptive response of the body to the changing environment in order to overcome the dangers and to protect itself in the fastest time period.

Today, the scenario has changed substantially. We do not face life threatening situations like the primitive man. But the same response is evoked during situations which are emotionally threatening such as in the workplace, at home, etc. This sort of stress which does not find release in the 'fight or flight' scenario can be damaging for the body and the heart in particular. It can also lead to irrational behaviour such as alcohol and drug abuse, unnecessary irritation, anger and even physical violence. Essentially stress even today remains an adaptive response of the body.

STRESS AS A PSYCHOSOMATIC ILLNESS

Stress can also cause what has been loosely termed as psychosomatic illnesses. A student preparing for an important examination is naturally under tremendous stress. On the exam day, the student may suffer from exhaustion, fatigue, fever or bowel peristalsis (caused by the contraction and relaxation of the walls of the digestive tract). This is the effect of stress on the body. Many researchers on stress think that excessive stress suppresses the immune system and thus causes disease. The immune system is the body's armour against all external attacks and if the immune system is weak, the body may fall prey to many diseases.

Further, people with long-term stress have been found to age faster. It is common to hear people say 'What a stressful time I passed through. I aged ten years in a month'. It was an of expression, but now it is a fact known that stress does make people age faster. A recent study conducted by psychologists at the University of California established a definite link between stress and a person's ageing. They found that people living under stressful conditions end up with damage to the DNA of their immune system cells which is called mononuclear cells. This damage resulted in the person ageing faster than normal.

IMPORTANCE OF STRESS MANAGEMENT

Thus managing stress in our day to day life assumes importance when we realise that a large number of people today are suffering from hypertension by the time they are 40. Although stress and hypertension are not one and the same thing, there is a direct relationship between stress and hypertension in the sense that continuous stress can lead to hypertension.

A stressed lifestyle leads to serious health problems which will no doubt follow unless steps are taken to keep this under control.

The pressures of modern living takes its toll whether you are a successful executive shuttling between meetings or a school teacher or housewife, leading a more sedate life. Thus it is important to know how stress affects the body and how you can change your lifestyle subtly in order to keep stress at bay.

Scientists and psychologists have been studying this for many years. Almost a century ago, Harvard physiologist Walter Cannon found that the body has a specific response when faced with a sudden threat — the respiration, heart rate, blood pressure and muscle tension all rises. This has since been termed as the 'fight or flight response' or the 'physiological stress response' which sets into process a series of events in the body.

STRESS AND BODY CHEMISTRY

The first of such events is the release of a chemical called CRH by the brain. The CRH stimulates the pituitary gland to produce a molecule called ACTH. The ACTH makes its way to the adrenal glands which then releases a hormone called cortisol. Cortisol keeps up the sugar level in the body, thus giving it the necessary energy levels for quick action. The adrenal glands also produce epinephrine, which makes the heart beat faster and increases the respiration rate.

The heart beating faster raises the blood pressure and results in an increase of blood flow to the limbs. The increased respiration ensures adequate supply of oxygen to the blood making the muscles more active. The body is now ready to face any threatening situations.

Unfortunately in today's world although there are enough threatening situations which stimulate the body to go into a fight or flight scenario, the tension that the body builds up does not find a physical release as in the fight or flight scenario. This results in a number of adverse reactions. Firstly, continuous exposure to stressful situations results in hypertension or increased blood pressure. The body's immune system is weakened, the person suffers from digestive problems and ulcers, and many more related illnesses. In fact recent research has indicated that more than half of the ailments that people suffer from today, can be traced to stress.

The bowel peristalsis referred to earlier is a scientifically explained relationship between emotional upheavals and gastro-intestinal problems. In fact so significant is this that it can be observed on a brain scan. Acidity, irritable bowel syndrome and diarrhea are some of the digestive problems caused by stress. They generally do not respond well to normal medication. However, stress reduction often helps in controlling these symptoms.

STRESS AND HYPERTENSION

Medical science has proved that stress leads to hypertension. People who lead hectic lives are always under pressure to meet deadlines and targets, are invariably stressed and end up with hypertension. Once a person has hypertension, the only sure way of checking it is supervised medication. Even for a person with hypertension, managing stress will ensure he does not increase his hypertension. For a perfectly healthy person, managing stress will ensure he remains healthy for a long time.

Hypertension can also be genetic. Such people with a family history of hypertension must take all precautions to prevent this from ruining their lives. Controlling stress and hypertension is not very difficult provided its methods are understood and care taken in due time.

The most damageing aspect of hypertension is that it is a silent killer. Unlike other diseases hypertension gives no indication of its onset till it is too late. Uncontrolled hypertension can cause irreparable damage to important organs such as the kidneys and lead to complications like renal failure. A person suffering from hypertension often continues to lead his normal life without making any lifestyle changes to control the same, simply because he is not aware that he is affected.

A person may know that he is suffering from acute hypertension only after he has been to a doctor for some other reason. This is the reason why every doctor checks the blood pressure of all patients. To prevent this killer disease a constant vigil and repeated check ups are required especially if you are in the risk group. You may consider yourself to be in the risk group if you have a parent with hypertension, if you have a stressful job, if you are passing through emotional trauma or if you find yourself getting angry and agitated without much reason.

STRESS AND DIABETES

Diabetes is a curse to the modern society. In most cases it has reached endemic proportions. The World Health Organisation had estimated that in the year 2000 more than 171 million people would suffer from diabetes. To make it worse, this figure is expected to double by the year 2030. This disease cuts across all strata of society and countries.

Diabetes is genetic in nature, but it can still be classified as a lifestyle disease. In other words, the seeds of diabetes may be sown genetically but it is nurtured and developed because of a faulty lifestyle. Bad eating habits, a sedentary lifestyle, a stressful atmosphere are its contributers.

Diabetes is a silent killer. There is no wound, there is no injury and there is no pain. That may be the reason why diabetes has reached endemic proportions. Most people who are in the risk group and may even be aware of it, do not realise till it is too late that they are suffering from diabetes. This is precisely the reason why this disease is so dangerous.

The complications associated with diabetes are very severe. They include eye disease, vascular disease, kidney failure, diabetic foot ulcers, ischaemic heart disease, stroke, gangrene and so on. Organ failure is often associated with long-term diabetes.

It is a tragedy that ignorance can take such a toll on world health. The management of diabetes is not that complicated. Even before clinical intervention, diabetes can be kept at arms length by correcting the faulty lifestyle. Healthy and timely meals, an active lifestyle with exercise, walking and other activities, discipline in day to day matters and reduction of stress levels are often all that is needed to keep it at bay.

There is no doubt that once a person is diagnosed with diabetes doctor's advice and medication is of utmost importance. But the medication will not help unless the lifestyle correction is simultaneously carried out.

Thus the last word is that whether you are in the risk group or not, maintaining a proper lifestyle will ensure that you lead a healthier and a more satisfied life without the nemesis of ill health hovering around you all the time. A balanced diet, less fat and sugar, less meats and most importantly an active life with lots of exercise will keep diabetes at bay. These are all very minor correction in your faulty lifestyle, but taken together their impact can be huge and may well mark the difference between an healthy person and an unhealthy one.

HOW TO REDUCE STRESS LEVELS?

Now that the physiology of stress has been understood, it is easy to comprehend that stress is the body's response to a situation which is perceived as threatening. Logically, if you can train the body not to recognise such situations as threatening, the job is half done. The body will not go into a fight or flight mode and the release of hormones and chemicals will not take place.

Have a relaxed attitude

The most potent way of fighting stress is to have a relaxed mindset. A tense man is always on his guard. In other words, he is perennially in the fight or flight mode. Naturally he is a prime candidate for stress and all the related problems.

Train the mind to relax and not to get tensed at every situation. This can be effectively done by practicing relaxation techniques. Research has proved that relaxation techniques are one of the most potent weapons in fighting stress. In our day to day life it is practically impossible to avoid stressful situations. But you can learn to live with them. This is through mastering some relaxation techniques.

Deep breathing is an effective relaxation techniques which helps to lessen stress in stressful situations. Practicing the proper breathing methods, such as pranayam can go a long way in reducing stress. Deep breathing accentuates the intake of oxygen into the blood system and thereby improves the functioning of the body as a whole. Your grandmother's advice of 'ten deep breaths' before you act in a tense situation is absolutely correct. Conventional wisdom has, as usual been proved right by modern science and medicine.

Pursue a hobby

Another good relaxation method is to pursue a hobby. If you are a highly stressed person, it may be a good idea to have a hobby such as, gardening, painting, music, reading, etc. This will not only relax your system as a whole, but will go a long way in reducing your stress levels. In fact every person should have a hobby to pursue in his spare time.

Listening to music or playing an instrument is a beautiful hobby. Music has been known to enhance growth in plants and make them bloom better. Animals have also been attracted to the sound of music. The fragrance of musk emanated by musk deer shows a marked enhancement when music is played. Many fishermen in the Far East play music to lure fish. When I got talking to some fishermen in Korea, I came to know that this is regularly done to increase the catch and has proven effective every time.

Music lightens the atmosphere and transports us to a different world. There is music for every mood, for every person. Some people enjoy jazz; others relax with ghazals, while some chill out with rock music.

In other words, find something in life to uplift your spirits. Having a pet, gardening, painting, singing, reading, music and writing are all hobbies which have beneficial effects in mind relaxation. If you do not have a hobby, cultivate one.

Laugh your worries away

Perhaps the most potent stress buster is laughter. Develop a sense of humour. Some people are so humourless that they radiate grumpiness. Remember stress and tension are contagious. If you get tensed in a particular situation, your colleagues, family members also get tensed. There are people who radiate tension. Such people pass on their tension to others and spoil the whole atmosphere. Over a period of time, people start avoiding such people and they become isolated and secluded.

Such people should know that they are only destroying themselves with their attitude. No matter what the problem is, it is not the end of the world. Today things may be looking pretty bad, but there is a new tomorrow, when the sun will shine brightly, the darkness will lift and there will be light and joy all around. Let us lift ourselves in anticipation of that day, even in our darkest hour.

In such times a little bit of humour can go a long way in lightening up the mood. I have mentioned some of these points in the earlier chapter but will now repeat them in view of the importance of humour and positive thinking in our lives.

Of course there are some situations where any sort of humour is out of place. But in any ordinarily tense situation such as at home or at the workplace, injecting some humour can make things a lot better for all of us. A laugh, a smile, a pat, a few kind words, a joke, these are the things that bring out the best in us and in others. They reduce the tension and directly reduce stress. So learn to master the situation and lighten the atmosphere. It will do you a lot of good, to bring out the best in the people around you and generate a lot of good will in your favour.

The fact that laughter is good for health is so well documented that probably everybody knows about it. It is a strange fact that as you climb up the ladder you find the laughs disappearing. It is rare to come across a top boss in an organisation who shares a good laugh with his subordinates. The rule is for them to be strict and stern at all times. So much so that their faces perpetually take on a grouchy expression. One can imagine the mood in the organisation where the boss looks like he has permanently got off on the wrong side of the bed. Similarly at home, when one of the family members is in a bad mood and is grumpy, everyone gets affected. Where at mealtimes the prevailing mood used to be one of well being, even if one member gets the blues, it affects all. This is because, tension, like humour, is contagious and spreads fast. Even if you are feeling good and optimistic, the sight of a pessimistic and eternally grouchy colleague is sometimes enough to smother your own good mood.

Avoid being grumpy

HRD experts have done many researches on this and have come with the probable reason why people are grumpy is because they are insecure. They fear that by laughing and joking with their subordinates, they are putting themselves on an equal footing with the subordinates and later on may not be able to control them. They further fear that the subordinates may take advantage of their good nature.

In short they lack the necessary skills to control the situation. A good leader should be able to control the situation at all times and should be able to exercise this control whenever he pleases. Grouchy bosses with grumpy faces lack the confidence to mingle with the crowd and thus their expression is that of a self-imposed barrier. But they forget that this acts as a barrier in communicating within the organisation, which in the long run affects the working, the output and ultimately meeting the deadline of the organisation.

Have an optimistic view on life

Be optimistic. Optimism gives us handsome dividends, no matter what the cause of our sorrow may be. By being grumpy, grouchy and a pessimist, you are spoiling your own health and happiness. Optimistic and happy people radiate joy and happiness, whereas cynical and grumpy people pollute the atmosphere with their bad vibes. Positive thinking has many benefits and a positive thinker is less prone to depression and stress than someone who thinks negatively. A positive thinker tries to look at the positive side of things and thus they do not affect him to a great extent. On the other hand a negative thinker starts brooding over his problems, compounding them and his health suffers as a result.

Everyone has been through situations which have seemed extremely painful at that time. Slowly as time passed, you overcame the bad times, you changed yourselves to adapt to the changing environment and slowly the bad memory also fade away.

In your darkest times you have to keep reminding yourself that even this shall pass, and a better, brighter tomorrow will dawn when you would have overcome your present difficulties and end up becoming stronger and better for it. Remember the darkest hour is just before dawn. 'When winter comes, can spring be far behind?'

You have to, therefore, maintain a proper perspective and be able to laugh at life's events rather than succumbing to them. It has been proved over and over again that laughing is good for health. So, buck up, crack a joke, have a good laugh and take life with a pinch of salt and a whole lot of laughter.

Women generally conduct stress better

As Judy Foreman writes in *The Boston Guide* :

"Scientists studying the body's response to stress have long focussed in the 'fight or flight' model - that animals sensing danger release hormones that speed things up, to either fight foes or flee, fast. But this view is incomplete, says Shelly Taylor, a University of California, Los Angeles, psychology professor. Her theory is that women have a potent stress fighting system based partly on oxytocin, the 'cuddling hormone'.

Oxytocin is known to be produced in women during childbirth and lactation, it has shown to boost bonding in rats, sheep, etc. And one study shows that giving male and female rats daily shots of it cuts the blood pressure and the stress hormone cortisol while promoting wound healing and, possibly weight gain.

Though women's blood may not hold more oxytocin than men's, it does have more oestrogen, which increases the available oxytocin's effectiveness. To Taylor and others, this shows that women may naturally cope with stress not just by fighting or fleeing, but by finding comfort in friends, too." .... As reproduced in Readers Digest.

Reach out to friends

Friendship is an important facet of human life. Talking to friends and discussing problems with them helps to reduce the stress of daily living. Man is a social being and blooms in the right company. That's why in every prison the most dreaded punishment is the 'isolation chamber' where the prisoner is kept isolated for days on end till he is a broken man, unable to fight any more.

Make friends. Remember in today's world nobody has time for another, so the effort must come from you. Go out of your way to strengthen the bond with you friends. Don't think that because they are not responding to your friendliness the way you want them to, they are not worth the trouble. Over a period of time your friends will realise your value and seek you out in good times and bad. And remember if you stand by someone in times of need, the bonds of friendship grow stronger. Friendship can never be cultivated by being 'sunny day's friends'. These are friends who are with you for a good time. When the chips are down and you really need their time and company they are nowhere to be seen. Friends are of utmost importance both during good times as well as bad times. Never desert or forget those friends who are passing through a rough patch in life.

A happy family is a healthy family

An important stress buster is the family. Spend time with your family, watch your kids grow, play games with them, act silly, in short let your hair down when at home. I know of many top executives who treat their homes as an extension of their offices, where they hold total control. Not only this alienates their spouse, even the children tend to stray and become distant from their parents. All this results in bad vibes and bickering when at home and invariably raises the blood pressure. Such people tend to spend more time at the office. Even at home they can be found pouring over their files or the laptop or so engrossed in phone calls or the TV that they fail to register the presence of their family. This is a vicious cycle and leads to broken families. The first sign of this is invariably hypertension.

Strike an intimate bonding with your spouse and children and see how they reciprocate. The ensuing family peace and happiness will ensure that you are more relaxed even in your work place. Small things will probably cease to irritate you. Discuss your problems with your spouse and take collective decisions regarding everything.

Perfect way to a stressful life

Another major cause of stress is the wish to be perfect, to be the best, to be acknowledged as the numero uno in whatever we do. This leads us to perform more and more and get into a tizzy over small things which invariably go wrong. We build this unsustainable pressure on ourselves until we can no longer carry on. You must have heard of a number of brilliant professionals who have ruined their lives due to what is called 'nervous breakdown'. Nervous breakdown is the body's response to intense pressure. It is like a mechanical plant shutting down because of overload. These people have driven themselves so hard, that at some stage they have suffered breakdown, which in many cases is irreversible. And for every case of nervous breakdown that occurs there are thousands of cases of hypertension, which leads to health complications and affects people adversely in their old age.

The first step is to acknowledge that you are not perfect. Everyone cannot be supermodels, have biceps like Schwarzenegger, be brilliant like Einstein or strike it rich like Bill Gates. Of course there is no harm in trying and even succeeding partially, but to make it your life's only ambition and driving yourself crazy, is not the solution. At some stage you have to step back and let the race go on. Think that those nearest and dearest to you, they like you for what you are already, not what you are dreaming of becoming. So get on with life, take a deep breath and move on.

Yet another reason for a healthy lifestyle

Another important way to reduce stress is a healthy lifestyle. Eat a balanced meal, get some physical activity, exercise, get enough sleep and be positive. Most of our diseases can be directly or indirectly connected with our lifestyle. People who live moderately lead happy and healthy lives. People who live as if there is no tomorrow consume their entire stock of good health and happiness in a short span of time and live to regret it. Strike the right balance in life, avoid excesses of any sort, understand and come to terms that you are what you are. Have the right perspective in life; avoid flogging yourself to perform better and better.

These are no specific treatment for stress, because putting it very simply, there is nothing that can eliminate stress from our lives. We experience stress every single day and we have to learn to deal with stressful situations, not by running to a doctor, but by acknowledging it, and getting on with our lives. But, yes a little bit of fine tuning of our lives can definitely reduce the recurrence of those stressful moments and add more smiles to our day to day living.

In fact, lifestyle change is the only permanent cure for stress and hypertension. Lifestyle change does not cost much and with your new moderate lifestyle you will probably save a handsome sum which you previously used to blow up at the restaurant, bar or club. In addition your body will respond by being healthier, trimmer and fitter. Thus there is no reason why people should not adopt a moderated lifestyle. It is good for the body, reduces fat, is easy on the wallet, keeps diseases such as hypertension and heart related diseases at a distance and brings the family closer. People with moderate lifestyles are invariably healthier and happier.

Now for some good news. According to Dr. Hans Selye, who studies the effect of stress on the body says that humans should not avoid stress. He is of the opinion that challenges in life if met and dealt with may actually be good for us. Studies on the effect of stress on humans have found that people who go through stressful experiences and are able to do well can survive any situation in life. Manageable stress boosts the immune system. Further, the body produces adrenaline and cortisol in response to stress. These hormones have a positive effect on the body and improve the memory. But one thing is for sure, continuous stress is harmful in the long run.

(As published in Readers Digest)

One of the most potent weapons in the fight against stress and stress related ailments is the mind-relaxing technique. Since stress is mostly in the mind, if you learn to relax your mind and not get worked up over every small issue, the battle against stress is half won.

SOME MIND RELAXING TECHNIQUES

Scientists, doctors, psychologists and ordinary people the world over are slowly waking up to an important force within our body which can be harnessed to fight diseases, improve memory, drive away depression and increase will power. This is known as the **power of the mind**. Nature has gifted every human being with extraordinary skills and the mind is the most important.

For years doctors have been resorting to 'placebo therapy', the use of placebos in hypochondriac patients. Fresh research in this field suggests that people who report improvement are not imagining that their pain and symptoms have reduced, but that placebo therapy gives specific results due to changes in the brain and body chemistry.

There are various ways to harness the power of the mind. Very often requires nothing at all, but to just sit back once in a while and allow the mind to take over. All the below techniques mentioned utilise the power of the mind and the body to help you to live a better life.

Meditation

Meditation is an important tool to fight stress. In India, meditation has been practiced for many thousands of years by sages and rishis. It is only now that meditation has been recognised as a potent mind relaxing technique and promoted as such. The benefits of meditation are numerous and is well-known and documented over the years.

Unfortunately most people are unable to master the technique of meditation. Although it is not difficult. Meditation is simply a procedure to train and tame the mind. There are many ways to meditate. These would help you to relax, chase away the blues and lower your stress levels. In case you are a highly stressed person and unable to meditate as explained here, you can opt to join one of the meditation centres and get professional help.

To practice meditation on your own, find a place where you will not be disturbed. Remember that a sudden noise or shock during the meditation can be harmful. Thus meditation is best done in an isolated place such as a closed room or in an open place which is not frequented. The sound of birds twittering, leaves rustling are good for meditation as you will then feel one with nature. As you practice and get the hang of meditation, you will find that you can cut out external sounds and distractions and do not need a closed room. Sitting is the most convenient position for meditation. It is recommended to sit straight in the crossed legged position with hands folded on the lap. This will make the bio-energic field of the body more compact and thus more intense.

Start with a few pranayam exercises. This is important as it gives the brain the essential oxygen to work clearly. When you meditate, breathing becomes slower, heart beat reduces and the body slowly slows down its speed of operation. The pranayam gives the body the extra oxygen required for this period.

Next close your eyes and let your mind drift. Concentrate on each and every thought that crosses your mind. Think of the mind as a playful monkey and your job is to tame this monkey. The way to do this is to stop at every random thought and study the thought. Soon you will notice that it is easier to concentrate on these random thoughts. As you gain experience in meditation, you will be able to isolate each thought and remove it before proceeding to the next thought.

The final hurdle is the time when these thoughts stop coming altogether. You have now mastered your mind and when you meditate you can instantly banish all thoughts from your mind and be one with the universe. This is what is known as the state of nirvana when you become completely blank. Meditation has been often described as "listening to the silence between thoughts". With practice you will be able to increase the period of silence.

The next step in meditation is thought analysing. Now that you have learnt to banish every thought from your mind, you can recall a particular thought and analyse it. This is the ultimate step in meditation and requires years of practice to be successful. Gautam Buddha was perhaps the greatest thinker to have mastered the art of meditation. Many great philosophers meditate in this way and examine deep philosophical ideas during meditation. In fact due to the popularity of meditation, even corporate honchos have taken up meditation and found this technique to be a successful problem solving tool.

The use of a mental sound is often helpful during the meditation. The word 'ohhmm' is considered ideal as it generates good vibrations within the body. Such a mental word is known as mantra. As you practice with the mantra you will notice that you become tuned to meditate as soon as you start the mantra. This is a good tool in times of distress when you can calm the mind very quickly by chanting the mantra a few times.

Meditation reins in the mind. Once you have practiced meditation you will notice a marked increase in your level of concentration. You will be able to register more deeply what others are saying. You will be able to absorb more of what you read, your logical reasoning powers will increase enormously and your mind will stop wandering.

Meditation is like giving the mind a 'break' from its 24 x 7 schedule. People who meditate are able to face life more confidently and solve their problems. Even physical health improves through meditation and the ageing process can be reduced. But the most important use of meditation is when you are passing through a crisis and the mind is in a turmoil. During such periods it is possible for the mind to go completely berserk and the person to suffer a nervous breakdown. Meditation will ensure that the mind remains in control of itself. The problem can be dealt with in the silence of meditation and the person comes through stronger and ready to meet life's challenges.

Like all mind-relaxing techniques, meditation is an exact science and is best practiced under the guidance of an instructor.

Improve your breathing technique

It has long been known to practitioners of yoga that systematic breathing held one of the keys to a healthy lifestyle. Pranayam is the one of the foundation pillars of yoga. There are many types of pranayam. Nowadays there are many gurus on television imparting sessions on pranayam. But as long as you stick to the basics there is no reason why you need a guru for this.

The basic concept of pranayam is to get rid of the stale air in the lungs. Most people breathe shallowly. Thus only 20 to 30 percent of the air is emptied out from the lungs during breathing, resulting in stale toxic air remaining in the lungs at all times. By practicing pranayam for just a few minutes daily, breathing deeply becomes a way of life and there is always plentiful oxygen-rich air in your lungs.

Oxygen is the source of life. Oxygen helps the tissues to grow and regenerate, while retarding the degeneration process. Thus it is good for both young and old. Pranayam has been known to alleviate serious problems and is a useful tool for all ages. The best part is that you can do it anywhere, anytime, without any expensive clinics and gurus.

Pranayam was known to our ancient ancestors and they often practiced pranayam in tandem with other forms of yoga and meditation. The role of oxygen in tissue generation, blood purification, disease fighting, etc., was known for thousands of years and pranayam is the technique to ensure plentiful supply of oxygen to the body.

The idea is to inhale deeply and to exhale deeply instead of 'shallow breathing' The purpose of pranayam is to train the body in the art of deep breathing using the stomach to push up and down on the diaphragm as required, thereby increasing the inflow and outflow of fresh air into the lungs.

A person who has mastered the art of pranayam will use it even in normal life. This is the aim of pranayam - to train the body to breathe deeply.

Hypnotherapy

Many doctors treating chronic patients of long-term stress refer them to a hypnotherapist. The therapist let you enter into a hypnotic state which relaxes both the mind and the body. Hypnotherapy is an accepted treatment to relax the mind and thereby lower stress levels. Once you are trained in hypnotherapy you can use this sort of treatment whenever you feel the tension within yourself rising.

But there are two points worth remembering. Hypnotherapy is a skilled science and the technique must be learnt from a trained therapist only, under the advice of your doctor. Secondly once you have learnt the technique, never fancy yourself to be a therapist and try to treat others. Untrained therapists with the wrong techniques can have a devastating effect on the minds of patients. Hypnotherapy is not a game. Remember, hypnotherapy is uncharted territory and is not to be practiced by laymen. Even in the hands of professionals, serious problems have taken place. So once you are participating in hypnotherapy, you are virtually handing over the keys of your mind to a stranger who may manipulate this for his own interests.

Personally I would not encourage any form of hypnotism, whether self hypnotism or through a therapist. Strange are the ways of the mind and we have not yet mastered the workings of the mind, hence it is better not to tamper with it unnecessarily.

Progressive muscle relaxation

It is a good way to not only relax your muscles, but also to relax your mind. It is especially useful after exercise, for then you can use it to relax both mind and body. It is a relatively easy and harmless procedure. You can lie flat on your back and concentrate on each part of your body or muscle group. Make an effort to relax the muscles involved. Then flex the same muscles and hold for a few seconds. Now relax the muscles and remain in this state for a few seconds before moving to the same part on the other side of the body.

Start with your toes. Do the left one first and then switch to the right. Try to concentrate on the part you are relaxing. After the toes, move on to your ankles, then calves, knees, thighs and upward, all the way to your shoulders, neck and head. The most important point here is that you have to imagine yourself to be in the part that you are relaxing. If you seriously want to practice progressive muscle relaxation, you must first rid your mind of random thoughts and then concentrate. The effects can be felt immediately if you are doing it the right way.

Since progressive muscle relaxation is a technique, it is good for people of all ages and can be effective for those who have sedentary jobs that involves sitting for long hours. It is also a good technique when you are on a long flight and have to sit in a cramped position for hours at a stretch.

In other words, progressive muscle relaxation is a method of relaxing the entire body by concentrating on a particular part at a time. It requires a bit of practice to master this art, but once you have learnt it, you will find it helpful in driving away fatigue at a short notice. It is totally harmless and promises quick results.

Mindfulness-based stress reduction

This treatment is currently the rage in parts of the US. It was developed by Jon Kabat-Zinn at the Center for Mindfulness in Medicine, Health Care and Society at the University of Massachusetts. This treatment has its origins in the Buddhist philosophy. Buddhist monks have long known to both practice and treat others with this form of therapy. The basic concept is to make the mind an objective observer of the chaos within itself. This form of treatment makes you more detached to the ongoing struggles within yourself. As Kabat-Zinn puts it, the objective is not to reach nirvana, but to observe the chaos in a compassionate way, 'like bubbles forming in a pot of water or weather patterns in the sky'.

Mindfulness-based stress reduction is unknown in India, although there are a couple of clinics offering this in Mumbai. It's effectiveness is documented but the actual effectiveness depends on the therapist and the willingness of the patient. The cost of such a therapy is prohibitive and is possible only for the very rich who can afford such luxuries.

Cognitive Behavioural Therapy (CBT)

Cognitive behavioural therapy is an exciting new non-medicative mind relaxing technique which focuses on the mind's internal strength to overcome various stress related problems and difficulties.

Studies have found this to be effective in dealing with various conditions such as depression, anxiety, panic attacks, phobias and so on. There are many practicing doctors who swear by CBT and who refer their patients to clinics offering professional CBT sessions. The therapist usually requires between 10 and 20 sessions to get to the root of your problem and provides solutions. The therapist delves into your life, fears, loves, ambitions and achievements and so on. It is in short a way to unwind yourself to a neutral third party and then see what exactly is worrying you.

Cognitive behavioural therapy is an extensive therapy which includes sittings with the therapist where you are made to understand his way of thinking and guided towards improving your cognitive skills thereby ridding yourself of the thoughts and fears stalking you. It enables you to openly discuss your fears and dreams with an outsider and then look for solutions to these issues.

The two most important pillars of CBT are :

- Altering ways of thinking – a person's thoughts, beliefs, ideas, attitudes, assumptions, mental imagery, and ways of directing his or her attention – for the better. This is the cognitive aspect of CBT.
- Helping a person greet the challenges and opportunities in his or her life with a clear and calm mind – and then taking actions that are likely to have desirable results. This is the behavioural aspect of CBT.

In the early stages of depression, panic attacks, anxiety insomnia or any similar problems, you can take advantage of cognitive behavioural therapy without visiting a clinic and hiring a therapist. This is why CBT is becoming popular around the world. Since it is a method of solving your own problems and coming to your own conclusions, it is highly acceptable to society. It can be practiced anywhere. There are no side effects, no medication, no stress on the mind or body. All it needs is for you to introspect yourself and come up with your own solutions.

Thus, you can be your own therapist and cure your own problem. Next time you feel depressed and reach out for that anti-depressant pill, hold yourself and do a self check. There are no expenses involved, no time wasted, all it requires is for you to be honest with yourself and follow the decisions taken by you. This is the reason that CBT is becoming more and more acceptable all over the world as the instant self help guide.

Making such a reality check will help you to focus your energies in the direction which will help you to overcome your worries and anxieties. But the catch is the implementation of the final decision. Remember, making a change in your way of thinking, changing your behavioural patterns, changing your lifestyle requires a lot of dedication and will power. But success is assured, provided you are true to yourself. You have nothing to lose. Give yourself three months with this system. During these three months, control your emotions, keep off the anti-depressants and sleeping pills, look at the world with a positive attitude, be a true friend, be a good listener and foremost lead a balanced life. You will find your worries disappearing and you will emerge as a confident and dynamic person.

Get started

All it requires for you to do your own CBT is to find a quiet place, a pencil and a sheet of paper. But remember for CBT to be effective, you need to examine yourself first and then write honestly.

- What is worrying you? Write down the three most worrying aspects of your life that makes you depressed.
- Write down the effect of each of these worrying thoughts on you – emotionally, physically and otherwise.
- What can you do to alleviate these worrying thoughts and make them go away.
- What is the likely effect of your actions – Is it going to be effective?
- Thus which action should you take?

A sample of such a sheet is given below :

Nature of worry	Effect of these	Actions to alleviate	Effect of actions	Final decision
No promotion	1. Reduction of self worth. 2. Effecting normal thinking process. 3. Tired, depressed and fed up.	- Work harder - Talk to the boss - Look for another job	- Since already working hard, may not help. - Talking to boss may help, especially if I get to talk to him and explain my situation.	1. Talk to the boss. Explain my contribution to the team and ask for a promotion. If not, find out why not. 2. If boss unrelenting, look for another job, but leave this job only after confirmation of the next job.
No friends	1. Feel incomplete 2. Feel lonely 3. No social activity hence depressed 4. Reach for the bottle	- Make friends in the workplace and in the neighbourhood. - Make a list of likely future friends. - Make an effort to be friendly and helpful.	- Mostly friendless because I keep to myself. Thus an effort on my part will be probably helpful. - Can give it a try.	- Make a list of likely people to be friendly with both in the workplace and in the neighbourhood. - Try to be friendly without being overbearing

				and fawning. - Shortlist two or three people who reciprocate
I am obese	1. Feel inferior to others. 2. People laugh behind my back and pass comments. 3. No friends. 4. Depressed and lonely.	- Try to reduce my weight. Make a concentrated effort at weight reduction. - Be normal with people. No need to be ashamed of being fat. - Be cheerful and friendly. Being gloomy because of this will not help matters.	- Reducing weight will surely help matters. - Must be cheerful and friendly whether I am fat or not. - Forget the comments people make, thinking about it will make matters worse.	1. Reduction of weight likely to be the most effective action. 2. Will give myself three months to reduce my weight by natural means of balanced diet and exercise, including walks, etc. 3. If I fail in three months think about taking professional help. 4. Must be normal and cheerful at all times.

For the above self therapy to be effective, remember to be brutally honest with yourself regarding your condition. First you have to analyse your condition and understand clearly that you are indeed going downhill. Next you have to find out what is troubling you. The mind is like a giant computer which sometimes hangs. The thought processes intertwine into one another and it may at times be difficult for the person to pinpoint what is it that is causing the bouts of depression, panic, anger, etc. This is where you have to talk to yourself and find out what is wrong with you. Once you admit that something is wrong you are already halfway on the path to improving your condition.

Face your problems – do not run away from them

Most people with such problems go into self denial that there is something wrong with them. This is a wrong signal to the mind and will escalate your problem. You are the first and last person to know and to deal with your problem. No therapy, no amount of reading, no medicines, no therapist and no doctor can cure you unless you want to cure yourself. Writing down your worrisome thoughts and fears is one of the best ways to acknowledge your problem and deal with it.

So next time you feel depressed, have suicidal thoughts, get angry with yourself or others, or feel panicky and start shaking, don't reach for that bottle of pills. Take a grip on yourself, take a few deep breaths, sit down, analyse your condition and write them down as explained. Then try to implement the actions you have written with all your will power and vigour. You will find that you can indeed overcome your condition and come out a stronger and more capable person.

Needless to say the full effectiveness of CBT can be realised only when it is conducted under supervised conditions under the guidance of a therapist. The therapist comes to understand your feelings and worries, know what's bothering you and takes the worries and phobias out of your system much like a psychiatrist. What we are attempting is a sort of self CBT and it should be clearly understood that it will never be as useful or effective as CBT done by a professional therapist.

Conducting one's own CBT is much like going on a thought finding mission inside your brain, digging those thoughts that are bothering you and making you behave in an irrational manner, then writing down your own solutions to the problems posed by these wayward thoughts and incidents. CBT done on your own is a harmless exercise in self prognosis and often helps you by pinpointing the problem as well as the solution. So you can give it a try, but if you are unsuccessful and keep getting depressed, panic attacks, etc., do go in for professional help so that your condition can be treated medically at the earliest.

LIFE-CHANGE INDEX

Life-change index is a concept used to analyse the amount of external stress that individuals are subjected to. It is a given fact that every external stimuli acts on us in various ways. Some give us pleasure, some pain. But almost all have some effect on our mental process. When something unpleasant occurs, we get stressed. This causes a chain of reaction, explained earlier, ultimately leading to depression, hypertension, heart disease, etc. A clear understanding of what brings on these changes will help us to overcome the effects.

Life-change index lists the various events that can have an effect on our mental makeup and causes stress. It is often used by professionals treating persons suffering from extreme stress to determine the cause and hence the treatment of the patients.

The self evaluation list below is provided at the Holistic Stress Control Institute on their website. Take the test to determine your individual stress exposure. Like all self evaluation tests, this one too has to be done with all honesty and careful consideration in order to get the best results.

Event Impact Score

Death of spouse --100

Divorce --73

Marital separation ---65

Jail term --63

Death of close family member---------------------------------63

Personal injury or illness---53

Marriage ---50

Fired at work--47

Marital reconciliation --45

Retirement---45

Change in health of family member -----------------------44

Pregnancy ---40

Sexual difficulties ---39

Gain of a new family member ----------------------------------39

Business readjustment---39

Change in financial state --------------------------------------38

Death of a close friend --37

Change to a different line of work---------------------------36

Change in number of arguments with spouse -----------35

Mortgage or other loan--31

Foreclosure of mortgage or loan -----------------------------30

Change in responsibilities at work --------------------------29

Son or daughter leaving home --------------------------------29

Trouble with in-laws--29

Outstanding personal achievement -------------------------28

Spouse begins or stop work------------------------------------26

Begin or end school --26

Change in living conditions------------------------------------25

Revisions of personal habits -----------------------------------24

Trouble with boss--23

Change in work hours or conditions ----------------------20

Change in residence---20

Change in schools --20

Change in recreations---------------------------------------19

Change in church activities ---------------------------------19

Change in social activities -----------------------------------19

Change in sleeping habits ------------------------------------16

Change in number of family get-togethers----------------15

Change in eating habits --------------------------------------15

Vacation--13

Christmas or other major festival approaching ----------12

Minor violation of the law------------------------------------11

Directions : If an event mentioned above has occurred in the past year, or is expected in the near future, copy the number in the score column. If the event has occurred or is expected to occur more than once, multiply this number by the frequency of the event.

Scoring the life-change index

The body is a finely timed instrument that does not like surprises. Any sudden change or stimuli affects the body, or the reordering of important routines that the body becomes used to, can cause needless stress, throwing your whole physical being into turmoil.

The following chart will give you some idea of how to informally score yourself on social readjustment scale. Since being healthy is the optimum state you want to achieve, being sick is the state of being you most want to avoid.

Life-change Units	Likelihood of Illness in Near Future
300+	about 80 percent
150-299	about 50 percent
less than 150	about 30 percent

The higher your Life-change score, the harder you have to work to get yourself back into a state of good health.

(T.H.Holmes and T.H. Rahe. "The Social Readjustment Rating Scale," Journal of Psychosomatic Research. 11:213, 1967.)

Remember the lifestyle-change index simply guides you to what effects the events can have on your system. It does not tell you what to do to overcome the effects. We cannot change all the above events, but once we know the effects of the changes, we can try to reduce the impact.

Accept the realities of life

Many of the events causing illness can be controlled to a certain extent. But life has to go on and we cannot live a life dictated by the above. For example, the approach of Christmas or some other major festival may be a cause of stress to some. But the pragmatic person can reduce the effects by not paying too much attention to such an occurrence. You may find your friends making preparations to celebrate in a way that you cannot, giving expensive gifts, etc., to their loved ones, which you may not be able to afford. These cause a certain stress in you which builds up and ultimately takes its toll on your health. Here is where a practical reasoning will be of help. Instead of getting carried away with what others are doing, a little introspection will help you to stabilise yourself.

The saying *"Do your best and forget the rest"* explains the attitude you must adopt in such situations. There is no point fretting about what you cannot do. Think about what you can do, do it and get it out of your system. Once done, stop thinking about it and carry on with your life. This way of thinking will give you valuable returns in life. Be happy with life, with the way you are leading it. Of course you should not fall into complacency, because then there will be no improvement in your life. But to fret and fume about it will surely bring bad health in its wake.

So, just do your best in life and carry on living life to the fullest. This way you will learn to live a life of happiness and cheer without brooding over what could have been.

SLEEP

The best bridge between despair and hope is a good night's sleep. – E. Joseph Cossman

Sleep is the best restorer for the body. You need an average of seven to eight hours sleep in a day. According to Hans P.A. Van Dongen, Ph.D., who conducted a study at the University of Pennsylvania, sleep deprivation makes the brain fatigued due to a build up of a chemical adenosine.

In fact your sleep must be such that you can get up in the morning without an alarm. *'If you need an alarm to get up in the morning', says James Maas, author of Power Sleep, 'then you must be sleep deprived'.*

A good night's sleep helps to improve your memory too. A study conducted by researchers from the University of Chicago found that volunteers with adequate sleep had a better memory to remember a list of words than those who had not slept well during the night.

So cut out those late nights when you return home at two in the morning on a regular basis. Fix a routine wherein you get at least seven to eight hours sleep every 24 hours period and try to stick to this routine. Your body will then be tuned to the sleep pattern and you will notice an overall improvement in your health and energy levels.

Many people have sleeping difficulties, termed as Insomnia. Such people should avoid taking short naps. They should avoid any sort of physical activity before bedtime, avoid stimulating drinks such as coffee and tea before going to bed. It goes without saying that the bed should be comfortable. Having a warm bath before retiring and listening to music at bedtime may also ensure a good night's sleep. But remember, insomnia may be related to a medical problem. So, if it persists you are advised to see a doctor.

But drugs may not be the right answer for insomnia. Gregg Jacobs, an insomnia expert writes in his book '*Say Goodnight to Insomnia*' that Cognitive Behaviour Therapy also known as CBT may be more effective in treating insomnia. As he explains, basically CBT is the same old things - sleep at the same times every night, get up at the same time, use the bed for sleeping only and learn to relax. CBT teaches these relaxation techniques and educates people regarding the causes that lead to anxiety which is one of the major causes of insomnia. One of the myths about lack of sleep is the fact that everybody needs eight hours of sleep and getting any less is bad for health. As Jacobs writes in his book, sleep requirements are different for different people and you have to know and be comfortable with your body's requirements. Insomniacs handle sleep deprivation better than normal people, says Jacobs.

Ultimately if you lead a simple and balanced life wherein you are contended with your lot, not fall prey to temptations and vices, you will sleep well every night.

Success is meaningless if you can't sleep at night because of harsh things said, petty secrets sharpened against hard and stony regret, just waiting to be plunged into the soft underbelly of a 'friendship'. - Margaret Cho

POINTS TO PONDER :

1. In today's scenario with the various pushes and pulls of modern living, stress is considered to be one the major health problems.

2. Stress leads to hypertension and it has been found that most heart related problems begin with hypertension and stress.

3. Stress is a response of the body to life threatening situations and primes the body to fight in such conditions. But in today's modern world when we are bombarded with stressful situations day in and day out, due to work pressures, family problems or whatever, this response of the body can be detrimental to our health.

4. The most effective solution to avoid stress is not to take life too seriously. Easier said than done, but if you have a more relaxed attitude, you will find that stressful situations do not affect you as much.

5. While job and job-related problems are a reality of life, having a life outside your job will be of help in order to reduce stress. In fact you will perform your job better if you are less stressed.

6. One solution is to learn to appreciate life in all its dimensions rather than remaining fixated on your job, your ambitions and material gains.

7. Enjoy the simple pleasures of life, cultivate a hobby, listen to music, spend quality time with your family, these are some of the best and inexpensive ways to a stress free life and ultimate good health.

8. Be optimistic, look brightly at the future and have hope. That's the mantra to overcoming your present troubles and rise to a new dawn.

In conclusion it would be useful to remember that ego is a stressful feeling which destroys the fabric of the mind. It is a good idea to scale down on ones ego and adopt a more humble approach to life. To achieve this, pay attention to your thoughts and action and when you feel that you are being egoistic, scale down and let go of the ego. Remember you are not better off than anybody else; we are all in it together so why have an inflated ego. Egoistic people tend to get stressful and heart problems, mental instability, isolation in society, etc., may follow. Remember humility pays and humble people are not only calm and composed; they also enjoy good health and happiness, free of stress.

***

6
WEALTH MANAGEMENT

> *"If a person gets his attitude toward money straight, it will help straighten out almost every other area in his life."*
>
> *– Billy Graham*

An important constituent of any form of life management is the management of one's finances. There is an old saying *'It is easier to earn money than save it'*. Why is it so ?

Everyone spents years in college doing a professional or vocational course before taking up a job. On the job one perhaps works for a couple of years as an apprentice and then gradually works his way up. Thus, the process of earning money entails a lot of hard work and labour.

How many months, weeks, days or hours have you spent trying to grasp the basics of money management ? None! You have spent years trying to streamline your technique of earning good money and yet not a moment to learn the technique of saving.

That's why it is more difficult to save money than earn it. As the saying goes, *'there are no free lunches'*. If you want to save your hard earned money, you have to learn the right technique of doing so. And that entails a lot of reading, understanding, making notes and collecting information. This chapter will help you to get on the right track and you have to take over from there.

Save or live on credit?

First of all, let us see why you need to save money ! Why not live for the day, blow it all up and enjoy life while you can and the devil may take tomorrow.

It is with this logic that some people live in debt and enjoy a much better standard of living than what their current financial status entails. Nowadays it is so easy to live beyond your means and mortgage your future to our lenders. There are any number of credit card company's who have made it very easy to live like this. In fact this addiction of taking easy credit had built up to such an extent that the bubble has bursted and the entire financial systems all over the world has cracked.

This was due to the availability of easy credit doled out by indulgent banks in a mad rush to get ahead of competition. As a result, companies, individuals, even countries found it easy to live beyond their means. This bubble had to burst one day and it did. Welcome to recession, friends! This recession was caused entirely due men's greed and the propensity to enjoy a lifestyle beyond their means without a thought that a day would come when all loans would have to be paid back with interest. That day did come and the bubble did burst. The results are too well documented - banks collapsed, stock markets plunged, companies went under, individuals found themselves bankrupt and in many cases behind bars and even countries had to officially declare themselves bankrupt.

Fortunately, most humans do not fall into this category. Humans are different from other living beings. What differentiates us from others in our ability to think about our future and do something about it. Everybody knows about the industrious ants that collect food year around and build up a buffer stock, so that when the rainy season comes and they are unable to forage for food, they have enough to see them through. Humans also have the tendency to save for the rainy day. It may be a period of ill health in the family, child's education or marriage, or any situation which requires a sudden outflow of money. Rather than running around and borrowing at that time, it is better for us to have a kitty which can be utilised when required, and replenished during normal times.

Generally when you are young, you have a tendency to splurge and live beyond your means. This is understandable and acceptable. As you grow older, have a family and set certain goals for your life, your instinct to save becomes stronger and you try to look for ways and means to save. Unfortunately your knowledge of money matters may be poor (except for people in the financial sector), and you end up with your money sleeping. Your endeavour should be to allow your money to work for you and have it multiplied.

The best way to make your money work is to learn about the various avenues available for parking your funds and what they offer. This chapter only serves as a primer and should be treated as a stepping stone. Once you get started on the right track, you have continue to learn the new trends in the financial market and apply this knowledge to our savings, so that your savings become dynamic, moving with the times, instead of some sleeping, static beast.

INVESTMENT OPTIONS

Some options available for investments are as follows :

1. Liquid cash
2. PPF
3. Government bonds
4. Government securities
5. Bank deposits
6. Post office deposits
7. Gold
8. Company fixed deposits
9. Real estate
10. Non-equity based mutual funds
11. Equity based mutual funds
12. Company shares
13. Insurance

It is important to note that the options above have been randomly numbered. The choice of investments is dependent on the risk profile of the investor which we shall discuss below. The above list only serves to concentrate our attention on the different financial instruments available to us today. There may well be other, even more attractive investment avenues open to the investor.

Liquid cash

Liquid cash is strictly speaking not an investment as it does not earn much interest. Rather, it is a hedge against the day when you need the money in a hurry. Most investments have a lead period, i.e., it takes a certain amount of time before the money comes to you. Thus it is a good idea to have some money in your savings account which can be withdrawn at a moments notice. And today with ATMs, etc., liquid money is really liquid.

How much should you keep in the savings account. Too much, and the money is sleeping - not earning enough interest. Too less, and you may find that in a crisis it is not enough. Three to six times of your monthly salary is a good amount to have in your savings account. Once you have this amount just forget about it and start saving the overflow amount. There will be a time when you will be thankful for it.

Banks also offer short-term deposits at lesser interest rates which are as good as a savings bank account. Then there are smart accounts available where the money although kept in a fixed deposit can be withdrawn anytime if required.

But remember, never keep money in the physical form with you beyond what you would need in an emergency. Keeping a lot of cash at home is an incentive for crime. Nowadays with ATMs available everywhere, there is no need to keep excess cash at home. Keep the money in the bank and sleep well at night.

PPF

Public Provident Fund is a wonderful avenue to save money and to save tax. PPF gives you double benefit, i.e., the amount you invest in PPF can be deducted from your taxable amount and the returns are tax free.

If you are in the top tax paying bracket this turns out to be quite a big relief, because you are talking of a large chunk of your income tax being reduced due to this investment. Thus for tax payers this is one of the best investment opportunities, one which is as safe as money in the bank, which gives a decent rate of interest and one which is entitled for an income tax rebate.

At the same time you need not bother that the amount building up in your account is taxable or not - it is tax free !! PPF interest is exempted from tax. This is an additional boon, making PPF more attractive even for non-tax payers, who need not fear that their returns will be taxed. There is no other investment which gives you both an income tax rebate as well as tax free returns, except life insurance. The returns on PPF is higher than that on insurance making it really good.

There is only one catch in the PPF - there is an upper limit to the amount that you can invest every year. Currently this amount is Rs 70,000.

The PPF account is initially opened for a period of 15 years with an option to extend for a further five years and then another five years. It can be opened at any SBI outlets throughout the country. You have to invest atleast Rs 100/- per annum to keep the account going. You can invest a maximum of twelve allotments a year, i.e., once a month. That means you can either invest the entire amount in one go or divide it into twelve monthly installments. No other investment gives you this sort of flexibility or this sort of returns.

What's more, after the initial seven years you can withdraw upto 50% of the maximum amount in your account a year back or four years back whichever is the least. And the withdrawal is so simple, you just need to fill a form and within a day or two, the amount is credited to your account. There is no penalty, no reduced interest rates involved when you withdraw from your PPF account. The amount withdrawn is simply deducted from your account.

Of course with changing interest rates, the attraction of PPF may vary. But no matter what the interest rate, if the tax component is taken into account, PPF still stands out as one of the best investment avenues guaranteed by the government.

In fact in today's financial scenario when many financial instruments are south bound, PPF appears to be the only safe bet which gives an attractive assured returns free of tax!!! Mutual funds may give negative returns, company deposits may disappear if the company goes bankrupt, banks may close overnight, prices of gold may remain steady, but rest assured, nothing can happen to your Public Provident Fund.

There was a time during the boom years when company fixed deposits, mutual funds, etc., offered more returns. But the risk factor nowadays makes the PPF far superior as it has a zero risk and is a guaranteed investment.

My advice is, rush to the nearest SBI and open a PPF account there in your name and in the name of each member of your family. Whatever money you can save can be put in there. It is as good as money in the bank and earns a good interest, while giving you better returns. And over the years the amount grows due to the interest. Currently PPF accounts are earning an interest of 8 % which is pretty decent in today's scenario.

Government bonds and securities

Bonds are a risk free avenue for investment for those investors who are risk averse. A bond, whether issued by a government or a corporation, has a specific maturity date, which can range from a few days to 20-30 years or even more. Based on the maturity period, bonds are referred to as bills or short-term bonds and long-term bonds. Bonds have a fixed face value, which is the amount to be returned to the investor upon maturity of the bond. During this period, investors receive a regular payment of interest, semi-annually or annually, which is calculated as a certain percentage of the face value and known as a 'coupon payment.'

Government securities comprise dated securities issued by the Government of India and state governments as also, treasury bills. The Central Government securities are issued for a minimum amount of Rs 10,000 (face value) and in multiples of Rs 10,000. They are issued through an auction carried out by the Reserve Bank of India.

Bonds are issued by the central government, state government as well as public sector units and corporates. Bonds can be issued at par, which means that the price at which one unit of the bond is being sold is same as the face value. Alternatively, they can be issued at a discount (less than the face value) or a premium (more than the face value).

State governments raise money through state-development loans. Local bodies of various states such as municipalities also tap the bond market from time to time. Bonds are also issued by public sector banks and PSUs. Corporates on the other hands raise funds by issuing commercial paper (short-term) and bonds (long-term).

Banks are the largest investors in the bond market. In the low-interest scenario that prevailed, it made more sense for banks to invest in government bonds than to give out loans. Mutual funds, in order to capitalise on low interest rates, started a good number of debt funds that mobilised a significant amount of money from the investors.

Bonds issued by corporates and the Government of India can be traded in the secondary market.

Unfortunately bonds do not find much favour with the retail investors due to their low interest rates, long maturity periods and taxability. However, tax free bonds issued by the RBI / State Government generate a good amount of interest amongst the general public and can be looked upon as a safe investment.

Bank deposits

Fixed deposits in banks are one of the safest avenues to park your funds. It is safe, secure and reasonably flexible - you can withdraw it within a couple of days. Today the banks have come out with a number of fixed deposit schemes to suit the individuals' needs. There are recurring deposits, where you put in a pre-determined amount every month. There are simple fixed deposits where the money is locked up for a fixed number of years. There is the monthly income schemes where you put in an amount and every month the interest is credited to your savings account. Then there are a number of imaginative schemes which vary from bank to bank.

Visit your bank, find out which scheme suits your needs and open an account. The only disadvantage is that the interest is taxable at source. That means the bank will deduct the interest at source and give you a TDS - Tax Deduction Slip. But be careful when you visit these banks. Many of the banks have savvy investment consultants who more often than not guide you away from fixed deposits and into riskier avenues such as mutual funds etc. Always be aware of your risk profile. Once you have decided to invest in bank deposits to keep your risk profile intact, do not be coerced by smooth talking consultants into riskier investments.

To sum up, it is a good idea to have some amount in the bank as a fixed deposit as this also acts as a hedge, should you need the money at short notice. Remember there is a penalty for early encashment.

In today's financial conditions it is best to keep your hard earned money in reputed established banks. Keep the money in a bank who is into core banking, this way your money will be safer.

POST OFFICE DEPOSITS

This is another good investment opportunity.

There are many options when considering an investment in post office schemes. The main attraction of post office schemes is the high degree of safety. So, for the risk averse investor these schemes are ideal. At the same time they offer a better rate of interest than bank deposits. In addition, there is no tax deduction at source. This is highly advantageous because investors can calculate their own tax liability and pay tax accordingly, rather than have it deducted at source as is the case with bank deposits.

Another advantage is that most of these schemes have tax benefits as well which will allow the investors to reduce their tax liability. There are many attractive options available with the post office which the investors can choose depending on their needs.

The schemes available currently are as follows:

1. **National Savings Certificate (NSC):** This is a tax saving instrument which offers an interest rate of around 8% compounded half yearly. All investments in National Savings Certificate are entitled to tax rebate under Section 88 of the Income Tax Act. Interests accruing from NSC are entitled to benefits under section 80L of the I.T. Act. This is a good investment opportunity for the tax payer as it offers triple benefits i.e. Section 88 benefits, Section 80L benefits and non-deduction of tax, at source. In addition it gives a decent rate of interest coupled with a high degree of safety.

   Perhaps the only disadvantage is that it is not liquid. Premature encashment of NSC take a long time and is a tedious process. So, when you need it most, you may find that you are unable to get the cash in hand quickly enough. And by any chance if you lose the NSC certificate, it will take you a long, long time and plenty of hassles before you get a duplicate certificate.

   The minimum amount of investment in NSC is Rs 100/- There is no upper limit for investment. But remember there are limits of benefits under section 88 and 80L.

2. **Kisan Vikas Patra (KVP):** This is another good investment which offers an interest rate of around 8.4 % compounded quarterly. It offers the high degree of safety associated with all post office schemes coupled with a decent rate of returns. There is no tax deduction at source. There are no tax benefits. An investment in KVP doubles in about 8 years and 7 months. The minimum investment is Rs 100 and there is no upper limit.

   The advantage is the ease of investments in this scheme. You can buy KVPs in anybody's name. There are no laborious forms to fill, no documents to be produced. The other obvious advantage is the decent rate of return coupled with the high degree of safety.

   KVPs are more liquid than NSCs. You can break the KVP and get your money in hand within a short time. The disadvantage is that should you lose your certificate, you might as well as bid your investment good bye as it is freely encashable .

3. **Monthly Income Scheme:** This is a deposit which gives you monthly returns. The interest rate is 8%. The period of deposit is 6 years, at the end of which a maturity bonus of 10% is given. There is no tax deduction at source, which makes it very convenient for those not in the tax bracket. Returns are entitled to benefits under section 80L of the Income Tax Act.

   This is an attractive scheme, specially for those who are risk averse. It gives a better rate of interest than banks and offer a high degree of safety. Again the non tax deduction at source, unlike in banks, along with 80L benefits makes it ideal for pensioners and small investors. The maximum you can invest in a single A/C is Rs 3 lakh and in a joint A/C is Rs 6 lakh. The minimum is Rs 1000.

   There are basically no disadvantages to speak of, other than the fact that a premature encashment may take some time. This scheme is ideal for the retired people who have some money in hand and want to invest with the intention of getting a monthly return.

4. **Recurring Deposits:** This is an ideal investment opportunity for tax payers and those outside the tax net. Many housewives routinely save a part of the money saved from household expenses in recurring deposits. There is no tax deduction at source and the returns are entitled to benefits under Section 80L. The rate of interest is around 7.50% compounded quarterly. The tenure is for 5 years. The minimum investment is Rs 10 p.m. and there is no upper limit. The advantage of a recurring deposit is its ability to quietly build up unseen. A recurring deposit best demonstrates the power of compounding. Before long the years would have rolled by and you

will find yourself sitting on a neat deposit thanks to your humble recurring deposit.

5. **Term Deposits:** These are almost the same as bank deposits, offering an interest rate of between 6.25% to 7.5%. The advantage is that there is no tax deduction at source and the returns are entitled to section 80L benefits.

   Thus this is a good avenue for the non-tax payer as well as the salaried tax payer to park their funds, and pay income tax on actuals, rather than tax deduction at source. These time deposits can be made for 1, 2, 3, 4 or 5 years. The minimum amount is Rs 200/- and there no upper limit.

6. **Senior Citizens Savings Scheme:** This is basically a scheme under the Government's senior citizens welfare programme. This scheme offers a better rate of interest of at least ½ to 1 % above the normal interest rates. There are no tax breaks and no deduction of tax at source. The tenure is for 5 years. The minimum investment in this scheme is Rs 1000 and the maximim Rs 15 lakh.

   An ideal investment opportunity for those above 55 years, this scheme is also available with public sector banks.

   Please note that the interest rates are variable and depends on the governments interest regime. The investor is advised to check the actual interest rates of individual schemes before investing.

   As a last word, investment in post office is recommended for many reasons. Firstly, you will develop the investment habit. Secondly, the post office is a smaller place and probably a friendlier place than the huge banks. Thirdly banks do not offer much of a variety of investment avenues. In a bank you will usually be restricted to either a fixed deposit or investment in mutual funds, etc. But the post offices have several schemes which may suit your requirement. Lastly post office deposits are not subject to tax deduction at source. Thus if you are in the non-taxable bracket, you can avoid the hassles of filling up various forms, etc., at the bank. Even if you are a tax payer, non deduction at source gives you the choice of tax planning and paying tax later if you find that your investments are indeed taxable. Lastly, most of the post office schemes come with some tax rebate or the other. It would be well worth you while to investigate these avenues before walking into that swanky bank.

Thus it is advisable to park a certain percentage of your funds in those post office schemes which suit you needs. The market may go up or down, banks may crash, real estate values may plummet, but you can depend on the post office to give your money back under all circumstances.

Company fixed deposits

Most companies accept fixed deposits. They use this money to enhance their cash flow. Generally the interest offered on these company deposits are higher than bank interest. Then there are financial companies which take money from you to and invest it on their own. These offer you slightly more than company deposits.

The company deposit route is a good way to squeeze a little extra from your investments. But it is important that you invest only in frontline companies which have AAA+ rating. There are many companies which offer substantially higher rate of interest. These are to be avoided at all costs. Ask yourself why they are offering you more interest than the market rate. Simple - they are unable to raise money the ordinary way as these companies may not financially sound. If you happen to be enticed with the higher rate of interest and invest in these companies, my advice to you is get out as fast as you can and hope that they refund the money to you without problems.

There are innumerable instances where companies have not refunded the money to the investor at the end of the period. Thus it is important that you choose the right company to invest in. Be suspicious of any company which offers more interest than the market rate. Don't touch companies whose names you have never heard of. Invest only in those companies which have a large capitalisation. Such companies are not likely to pack up leaving you in the lurch. And avoid investing for a very long-term even though the interest rates may be more attractive. For example, if you think of investing for a 5-year period, forget it. Five years is a long, long time in the life of a company. Many things can change and you may find yourself unable to get your money back. Again, you own financial position may change and you may find that you need the money. Instead of breaking the deposit and losing out on the interest, it is better to go for a 2-year or 3-year term.

Always monitor the companies where you have invested in. Keep yourselves always upgraded and informed about the company's policies and financial status. Look out for news related to the companies where you have invested. And the moment you get the whiff of any bad news take your money out. Don't wait for the bad news to become a torrent, then you will find that everyone is rushing to take out the money and the company will be unable to meet this run on their deposits. So, the best policy is quit at the first sign of trouble.

Remember to put your hard earned money in good well-known companies, even if their interest rates are not the best. This list can go on, but the purpose of naming these three companies is that you can get an idea of the type of companies I am talking about. All companies do not always accept fixed deposits, you have to find out which companies are in the market for fixed deposits and then decide.

Most importantly do not be greedy. Many cash strapped companies who are unable to raise money offer interest rates of 5-10% above the market rate. Too often, investors flock to these companies and park their hard earned funds with them in the hope of squeezing out a few percentage points more. Soon enough many of these companies sink without a trace, unable to bear the high interest costs. Thus the greedy investors are left in the lurch.

MUTUAL FUNDS

These are the best option for the lay investor who wants to partake of the party in the equities market, but does not have the requisite knowledge and courage to do so.

Mutual funds take deposits from the public and invest these in equity shares of various companies. The investor buys units from the mutual fund at the current NAV - Net Asset Value. This as the name suggests is the value of the total assets held by the company in various investments divided by the total number of units sold. Thus it follows that in a bull market where the share prices are rising, the NAV also rises. Thus the investor's value goes up. When the investor wants to exit the fund, he simply sells the units back to the mutual fund at the existing NAV.

There are many type of mutual funds but the ones likely to give you the best returns are equity based funds. There is no doubt that in the long run investment in equities give better returns than any other type of investments. Thus you can invest in equities through mutual funds upto the limit allowed by your risk profile.

How do equity mutual funds work? They employ financial experts who study the market very closely and buy or sell their equities accordingly. Because of the fact that they invest in many companies at the same time, the collapse of a company or a slide in its shares for any reason affects the fund very little. But when the market as a whole is going down then obviously the NAV does get affected.

Most mutual funds have offices or agents in the cities who can be contacted for purchase or resale of units in these mutual funds. Many mutual funds offer two options - dividend or growth. This choice depends upon the financial condition of the investor. If the investor is currently in a good financial position, it is best to opt for a growth plan and allow your money to grow. But if you are looking at periodic returns then a dividend plan will definitely suit your requirements.

Choose the right fund

Nowadays there are vast assortments of mutual funds available in the market. In fact so much so that the choice of the right fund may be difficult for the lay investor. And mutual funds can be bought or sold online which increases their liquidity. Here a few basic points should be remembered while investing in mutual funds:

1. Check the past record of the mutual fund and the company. The particular one you choose should not be a start-up, but must be in the business for at least three to five years. Choose a company which is well-known in the market. Such blue chip companies are not likely to vamoose with your money. Nowadays most financial magazines carry details of mutual fund companies and their overall performance. Use this information to guide you in your choice. Some good mutual fund companies which have given consistently good returns are SBI, HSBC, Templeton, Alliance and so on.

2. The particular fund should preferably be in existence for at least 3 years and have a history of steady growth and dividend yield. Choose a fund that has a large corpus. A company which has a large amount of money invested in the fund is more likely to have their best brains in managing that particular fund.

Unless you know about the economy and which sectors are going to look up, choose a balanced equity fund. These funds invest the money in am assortment of companies and are less likely to be affected by downturns in cyclical sectors. Of course if you have reason to believe that a particular sector is going to outshine others, then go ahead and invest in a mutual fund servicing that particular sector. But keep a close watch on that sector and at the slightest hint of trouble, get out with your money, fast.

The performance of the fund should have been better than the stock market. In other words it should beat the sensex to merit an investment.

3. Read up on any and all articles dealing with mutual funds. This way you will be educating yourself and continuously updating your knowledge which is so necessary for sound financial management. Remember the mutual funds are just custodians of your money and are also liable to make mistakes. Track your funds regularly and exit if you are not satisfied with the performance or there is any adverse news about the fund or its prompters. It pays to be careful. Don't be taken in by the newsletters mailed to you by the fund managers. But spare a moment to look at the financial figures in these newsletters.

4. Lastly never invest all your money in one fund or in one company. Spread your risk across several funds of several companies so that the bad

performance of a single fund or a single company does not leave you high and dry.

5. Remember, the money is yours and the mutual funds are merely custodians of it. Thus it is your responsibility to ensure that they take care of your money. If you are in any doubt regarding the fund, it is a good idea to switch to another fund. If you do not have the time to track your investments it is a good idea to contact a financial advisor who will track your portfolio of equities, mutual funds, fixed deposits etc. and guide you through the tricky areas so that your money gives you the optimum returns.

EQUITY AND THE STOCK MARKET

This is the best avenue for those with an appetite for risk and looking for higher returns. The stock market is exhilarating, exciting, adventurous, risky and dangerous. It has the potential to make or break the investor. Anyone who wants to risk their money in the stock market must do so only if they have the requisite knowledge to ride the troughs and crests of the market. It is not the place for lay investors with no knowledge except what their brokers or friends tell them. Too many such people have had their entire wealth wiped out because of ill-informed decisions.

First of all an investor who wants to enter the market directly must educate himself about the various terms and definitions used. He should be aware of such terms as equity capital, RONW, dividend yield, Beta, OPM and many more which will help to study the underlying fundamental strength of the company. All decisions regarding which company shares to invest in must be made after a thorough look into the fundamentals of the company. Today there are many magazines available which give the complete financial details of the companies.

Retail investors like you and me must invest for the long-term. Short-term investments are risky and can give only little gains with a lot of risk. This risk might often result in a negative return.

Many retail investors burn their fingers by buying when the market is on a bull run, i.e., the prices are rising. Unless you are able to buy at the initial stages, when the market has not yet heated up, it is better to wait for corrections before buying. The stock market is a cyclical beast. It is the result of collective thinking of its many players. Thus an intelligent investor can predetermine when the market will rise and when it will fall. I am not talking about the day to day fluctuations or even the weekly ups and downs, but about the longer term. Thus if the market has entered into a long-term bull run, say, because of the state of the economy of the country, a few well researched shares with good fundamentals will give the investor very good returns in the long run. Similarly even during the bull run, the market enters into a correction phase, during which it may crash for a day or two, before resuming its upward march. An intelligent investor can use these correction phases to enter a bull market.

Similarly when the market enters a bear phase due to political turmoil, it is a good idea for the investor to sell his shares and buy them back when the market has hit the bottom. This way he has taken advantage of the drop in the prices rather than see the value of his investments dwindle.

This is called timing and is perhaps as important in share investment as the fundamentals of the individual companies. To get the timing right, the investor must have his fingers on the pulse of the latest news and the current financial trends. In other words a smart, savvy and intelligent investor can make money in the stock market. And what if you are not? Very simple, avoid the stock market and go for the mutual funds which have many smart, savvy and intelligent persons managing your funds for you! But it is important to remember that it is practically impossible to time the market with any amount of accuracy, thus the investor must use his logic on when to enter and exit.

Look before you leap into the stock market

The following points may be noted before you think of jumping into the murky waters of the stock market:

1. Assess your capacity for risk. See the paragraph under risk profile and decide for yourself how much exposure to risky investments you can withstand. Remember the stock market is one of the riskiest investments, at the same time the one with the maximum potential for gain. So, know your own risk profile and take an educated risk.

2. Invest in blue chip large cap companies. Companies with a large capitalisation have their own inherent strengths and although they will not dazzle in the market they will not collapse either. The market capitalisation of a company is the product of the market price of its shares and the number of shares of the company. It is better for the retail investor to bet on large companies. Once you have learned to ride the market you can venture into smaller companies, which have more potential for price escalation in a bull market. But remember mid-cap companies will not withstand if the market is in a free fall. Investment in smaller companies must be made with caution and these should form only a small fraction c the total portfolio. The fact is that brokers and financial institutions often play with the share price of these smaller companies, taking them to dizzying heights and then booking profits leaving the retail investors in the lurch.

3. Avoid very small companies and those known as penny stocks which have no intrinsic value. You will often find tips in various

magazines on how these shares are going to rise. Don't let you investment decisions be coloured with greed. Although it is true that some small companies may give astronomical returns, it is a big gamble all the way. And here you are talking about financial management, not about gambling. Thus as a rule stay away from such companies and do not be swayed by the so-called pundits who love to wax eloquent on the stock market in good times and do a sudden turn around when things start looking bad.

4. Study the fundamentals of the company before you decide to invest in it. Read about the company, see the financials, check the growth rate, assess the potential of the sector and industry. If you are satisfied all the way, go ahead and buy. But remember, constantly upgrade your information on these companies. Although I always say that the retail investor must invest for the long-term, if the fundamentals are deteriorating and the company is on the downslide, it is time to say goodbye to the share.

5. Don't fall in love with the share, don't lock it up in a trunk and forget about it. Too many blue chip companies have gone down over a period of time. By long-term outlook, I mean anything more than 1 year, not twenty years. Cycles change, economy goes up and down, companies change their management, market perception about a particular company changes and every one of these has an effect on the price of the share. Keep in touch and when in doubt, get out.

Check the fundamentals of the company

Now let us look at a few of the terms and how to identify the good fundamentals of a company :

1. **Face Value :** The face value of a share is its original value at the time of allotting the shares to the investor. Of course subsequently, if the company has issued bonus shares, then the face value will reduce. For example, the company issued shares at the rate of Rs 10 during the IPO. (IPO stands for Initial Public Offering, when the company originally allots shares to the investors). Five years down the line, the company decides to go for a split option. If the split is in the ratio 1:1 you will get one share for every share by you. The face value of the share will now stand reduced to Rs 5/-.

   The face value is important to the shareholder because the dividends are issued on face value. When the company declares a 50% dividend and the face value is Rs 5 then the shareholder gets Rs 2.50 for every share held. But if the face value were Rs 10 then he would get Rs 5 for every share held.

2. **Equity Capital :** This is the total amount for which the company has issued shares. Equity capital is a function of shareholder participation. Equity capital has to be seen in two ways. A smaller equity capital will mean that either the company is a fledgling, with not enough working capital, whereas the company with a larger equity capital has had more access to funds and thus would have expanded more. Again a company with a smaller equity capital would have relied more on loans from financial institutions, banks and the public through company deposits. Such a company will have a tremendous outflow through interests which will hamper growth. A company with a larger equity capital would have relied less on loans and thus the interest outflow is limited which will give it a larger capacity for growth and enhancing shareholder wealth.

   On the other hand a company with a larger equity capital will have more dividend outflow and thus the quantum of dividend declared would automatically reduce, unless the company has posted spectacular results for the year.

3. **Book Value :** The book value is the value of the company as it appears in its books. It has nothing to do with the market price of the company's shares. Book value is calculated by dividing the sum of the equity capital and reserves by the number of equity shares. Book value is a sign of the inherent strength of the company. There is a ratio called the price to book ratio which gives the relative strength of the company. The lower this ratio the more inherent strength the company has. For example, a company with a book value of Rs 50 and a price of Rs 50 has a price to book ratio of 1 and is a good buy provided the other fundamentals are also good.

4. **Return on Net Worth (RONW) :** This is an indication of how well the company is managing its resources and the returns it gets. It is arrived by dividing the net profit by the sum of the equity and reserves. In short a company with a low equity capital, which has posted a huge profit will have a large RONW. But if the company has a large amount of unutilised reserves, the RONW will go down as the reserves are not being put into effective use.

5. **Operating Profit Margin (OPM) :** This again is an indication of the company's operating efficiency. It is calculated by subtracting the Operating Expenses from the Operating Income and dividing this by the Operating Income. Some companies report a scorching OPM of 100 and is an indication of the operational efficiency of the company. The better the OPM the more efficient the company and the brighter its prospects.

6. **Earnings Per Share (EPS) :** This is the ratio of the Net Profit (less preference dividend) to the number of equity shares of the company. This figure is directly related to the returns that the investor can expect. For example, a company with a large equity base might post a huge net profit, but the fact that the equity base is so large dilutes the ultimate returns to the shareholder as the profits have to be shared by all. EPS removes this anomaly and gives the investor a better tool to estimate what returns he can expect from the company.

7. **Beta :** This figure indicates the share price movement vis-vis the index. In other words it tells us how sensitive the share price is to the index. A Beta of 1 indicates that the share price moves in tandem with the index. A Beta of more than one indicates a volatile share whose rise and fall may be disproportionately large than the market fluctuations. A Beta of less than 1 indicates a share which does not react much to market movement.

   Generally it is a good idea to invest in shares which have a Beta of one or less than one. The prices of such shares are more affected by the fundamentals of the company rather than market sentiments. Although in a bull run, these shares may not show a spectacular rise, at times, when the market enters into a bear phase, they manage to hold out and not get into a free fall like the more volatile ones.

8. **Price to Earning Ratio (P/E) :** This, as the name itself suggests is the ratio of the market price to the EPS. In other words, it tells you what premium the market pays for the share as compared to its earnings. If the market price of the share is say, Rs 120 and it EPS is 10, then the PE of the share is 12.

   The PE of a particular company can be compared to the Industry PE to get an idea of how the company is faring as compared to the particular industry as a whole. The industry PE is the sum of the market capitilisation of all the companies in that industry divided by the sum of net profits of all the companies in that industry (the preference dividend and the dividend tax, if any are subtracted from the net profits).

   A company whose PE ratio is substantially better than the industry PE ratio, indicates that the company is better run and more efficient. Thus this company has a better scope for future growth. But at the same time well run companies with a lesser PE ratio has a better scope for price escalation once the market perception about the company improves.

9. **Market Capitalisation :** This is the market value of the company. It is obtained by multiplying the market price of the share with the

number of equity shares the company has issued.

Generally a company with a market capitalisation of more than 1000 crores is known as a large cap company. One with a market capitalisation of between 400 to 1000 crores is a mid cap company, while those with a value below 400 crores are known as small cap companies.

The golden rule for the prudent investor - do not fall for the lure of small cap companies. Agreed some small cap companies have performed very well, but these are few and far between. These small cap companies are often used by operators to make a fast buck on speculation and thus they are more prone to folding up during bad times. Instead focus on large cap companies for your long-term investment. If you are willing to make a calculated risk you may invest in some good mid cap companies as kick starters for your portfolio after studying their fundamentals. On an average large cap companies must account for at least 70% of your total investments in shares. And remember, as you become older you capacity for risk reduces and therefore your exposure to large cap companies must increase as a percentage.

10. **Dividend Yield:** This is a most important figure for the retail investor. It is the percentage ratio of the dividend to the market price of the share.

This will show you how much your money is earning through dividends alone. It is important because if a company is giving you a dividend yield equal to or more than the bank rates, then you can really lock up this share in your trunk. It will not matter whether the share price is rising or falling, because anyway you investment is earning more then the bank rate. Thus before you invest in any shares have a look at the yield it offers. In fact any yield over 4% should be considered decent. Try to avoid those shares which offer a meager one or two percent yield. In such a case you are solely dependent on capital gains and in an extended bear market your investment will go to sleep. But if it offers a decent yield then, even if the prices go down, you can be secure in the knowledge that at least your investment is earning something.

Before you invest in the share market you must be aware of its fundamentals as mentioned above. No one point should sway your judgement. Your choice of shares must be made after considering all the pros and cons of each company. It is not an easy choice and there are no easy answers.

Selection of the best company to invest in

It takes a lot of hard work and research to home in on the right share to pick. For starters, shortlist the large cap shares. They are less likely to let you down when the times are tough. Then, select those with a higher than average book value and compare this with the price. A very high price to book value ratio means that the company's shares are over priced. From this list cut out the ones with a RONW (Return on Net Worth) of less than 15 % and an OPM (Operating Profit Margin)of less than 15 %. Next check PE (price to Earnings) ratio and compare this with the industry PE ratio. If the PE of the company is substantially above the industry PE this may mean that the share is overvalued. If the PE is substantially less than the industry PE, this may mean that the market players do not favour this company at the particular time. This may be treated as an opportunity to get a share at a reasonable price or it may be treated as a lack of confidence in the company's management.

From this select the ones with the higher EPS and lower Beta. These will not dance to the markets tunes all the time. Lastly, from the handful of shares that remain on your list, select those with a higher dividend yield. These are the shares that you should concentrate on and which will give you the best returns. Good Luck !!

Gold

Gold has long held a special charm for mankind. Because of its bright lustre, its malleability and its indestructibility, it has been considered valuable and commands a good price. Gold, or the 'yellow metal' as it is usually called, was the cause of man killing man, countries going to war and a whole lot of other crimes in the past.

Gold is one of the best avenues for investment at all levels. Many countries keep a good stock of gold to tide over bad times. When economies are down, currencies plummet, stock markets head south and interest rates drop, gold seems to be a steady and viable avenue to invest. That is the reason that gold commands a good price and is traded all over the world.

But does gold really give a good return? One of the most important factors in favour of gold is that its price rarely goes down drastically. In fact it is one of the rare investments that hold its own even in an economy on the slide. Thus it has attracted the interest of even the most savvy of investors.

Historically, gold has not been known to give a good return to the investor. In the long run, the stock market is a much more attractive investment opportunity. But the sad fact is that the stock market is fraught with insecurities. So for the unwary investor it could turn out to be a nightmare. Gold, on the other hand, is not susceptible to such wild swings. Thus many people consider gold to be an investment opportunity.

Yes, it is an investment opportunity, if you can disassociate emotionally from it. But usually the person who buys gold, does so in the form of jewellery. This has an emotional effect and even in bad times we are loathe to liquidate it. Thus it loses its value as an investment and becomes a liability.

If you do invest in gold as an investment it is necessary to think of it only as an investment and be ready to liquidate it without any emotional hassles. Then only will you get the right benefit from this steady source of investment.

But if you think of gold as an investment, invest in gold bars. Gold bars have reasonably good liquidity and the rate of return on gold has so far been good. This is mainly due to an increase in demand, especially in countries such as India, without matching supplies. Further due to the weakening of the dollar there was and still is an increasing interest in gold.

If for some reason or the other you don't want to get into the nitty gritty of buying gold whether in bars or coins, you can opt for a gold bond or ETF. Many mutual funds offer gold bonds or ETF, whose NAV is dependent on the price of gold. In short the NAV of the bond moves in tandem with the price of gold. Thus if the price of gold has gone up by 10% in the year that you have been holding the bond, you get a 10% return on your investment should you choose to exit the bond.

REAL ESTATE

Real estate in simple terms means property. Property has always held a strange fascination specially for Indians and it is always considered an achievement to have your own property. In rural India property is the cause of sensuaal murders. It is common to read of brother killing each other, sons killing their parents and neighbour's plotting against each other, all in the name of property. Ownership of property has an attraction for humans all over the world. The reason is not far to seek. Real estate is a safe immovable asset which shows a steady appreciation over time. The stock markets may crash, interest rates may go up and down, even the price of gold may fall, but property prices are rarely known to dip. Yes in euphoric times, when the stock market hit a bull run, the property prices may reach stratospheric levels. When the bull run is over, their prices may fall back to original price. This does not mean that the price has actually fallen, it means that the prices rode a crest and is now back to normal.

Thus real estate investments can give you a steady appreciation over the years. Secondly, by leasing it or renting it out you can double the returns. You get the rent on it as well as capital appreciation. Another advantage is that being immobile, your investment is always safe, Short of an earthquake, there are no chances of your investment disappearing if you have chosen carefully. Thirdly, you need not stay awake at nights worrying about the stock market, oil prices, the state of the economy or the dollar value. Your investment will always give you a good return in absolute terms.

Disadvantages of real estate as an Investment

Now the question is 'is investing in real estate a good option?' The answer is not an easy one. For, despite the obvious advantage of steady price increase, there are some major disadvantages involved in this investment. For promoters and business men, it may be a value investment, but for the common man real estate does not score high on the list of popular investment avenues.

The first and foremost disadvantage is that it is highly illiquid. Should you want to sell property in a hurry, you will find that it is not an easy matter. It takes anything from one month to over a year to sell off property at decent prices. Of course this period will be considerably lesser, in case you are making a distress sale, at prices that are below the market price. Thus when you are in dire straits and need some quick cash to tide over your immediate problems, real estate will prove to be of no help at all.

The second disadvantage is the formalities involved in the sale. Whether you are buying or selling, the formalities involved can be frustrating. For purchase of the property you have to get hold of all the documents related to it, and then go through them with a fine tooth comb. It is always better to employ a known lawyer to check these documents. Generally with most properties, one or the other of the documents may not be available, due mainly to the carelessness of the owners, who have probably misplaced the same. Once you have all the documents in hand and your lawyer gives you the green signal, the property has to be registered in your name. This involves more paperwork and time. All this can be pretty taxing if done repeatedly. Generally most of us purchase the property once in a life-time, that is our residence, so we can bear the trouble. But if this is to be done regularly as an investment, then it is better to have a professional do all the running around for you.

The third disadvantage is the fear of being cheated. There are innumerable cases where, the intended buyer paid the full price, or part of the price to the seller, only to realise that he was not the owner in the first place. In some cases the seller could not produce all the papers thus delaying the sale and causing financial loss and lots of problems for the buyer. There is a well-known case of someone having almost sold the Taj Mahal to a tourist! So if you want to buy any property, you have to be extremely careful and guard against being cheated out of your money.

Another disadvantage is litigation. You have purchased the property, paid off the seller and even registered it in your name. Suddenly you have someone popping up at your doorstep claiming that that he is the co-owner of the property. Such cases can mean a lot of unnecessary trouble and bother.

Thus keeping all this in mind, real estate is not on the top of my list of investments specially for ordinary people. The only exception is if you are buying property for your own residence or for the use of your near and dear ones. Real estate as a means of investment can turn out to be counter productive, if you are not really careful and know the ropes. But on the other hand, if you are savvy with the real estate industry and know your way around, then definitely it is a great investment opportunity and should be in your list of investments.

INSURANCE

Insurance is, strictly speaking, not an investment, but a necessity. Whether it be life insurance, accident insurance or insurance against specific diseases, one must be adequately covered against these calamities. Death and disease are a necessary part of life. We have to accept it gracefully and make sufficient provisions for it, so that when we fall victims, out loved ones do not have to go from pillar to post to find the means of treatment and survival.

Life insurance has become quite popular and well-known in India. Everyone who is the bread winner of the family must first adequately insure his life before thinking of other investments. This is because life is very fickle and no one can predict what can happen tomorrow. Thus it is better to be prepared and ensure that one's family has enough for basic subsistence when the bread winner is no more.

The question often asked is, how much to insure. There is no point in over insuring oneself, thus it is necessary to calculate what the monthly expenses for basic survival of the family amounts, taking into account educational expenses, etc. It is a good idea to insure for an amount equivalent to 72 times this amount. In other words enough for 6 years at current levels. In otherwords if you calculate your basic monthly expense as Rs 15,000 then as the bread winner of the family, your life should be insured for at least Rs 11 lakhs. For the purpose of this calculation, you can cut out the unnecessary expenses, but be sure to include the basic expenses, also known as daily needs. Add to this doctors bills, educational expenses and any other expenses you consider vital. The idea is that the family can continue to live without lessening their standard of living too much.

The figure of 72 months is reasonable because with inflation etc., this will come down to 60 months and 5 years is enough for the family to get back on their feet and be self sufficient. Nobody can bring back the person who is no more, but having this sort of basic cover will ensure that the family can live a life of dignity even after the blow.

Although life insurance is not an investment, the returns on the premiums are attractive enough for it to fall in this category. Today the rate if interest on premiums are in the range of 6%. All amounts paid as premiums for life insurance are eligible for tax rebate, subject to the upper limit under Section 88 of the I.T. Act. Further the returns on maturity or death are exempted from tax. So, assuming that the insurer survives the period, he gets the sum assured back, tax free. Thus life insurance is not only a cover for life risk, it gives you decent tax free returns.

Health Insurance

Next is health insurance. This is as necessary as life insurance, since it insures you against any major health problems requiring hospitalisation. Everyone must again, be adequately covered for this. Thus as old age comes on, you are confident that even if fate gives you a cruel blow and you are afflicted with any sort of illness, you will not suffer monetarily. The amount of health insurance depends on each individual, it is an annual premium and you get the coverage for the diseases mentioned in the policy. Be sure to read the policy carefully, so you know where you stand. And remember to declare all pre-existing diseases. For example, if a person having a high blood pressure did not declare the same, the insurer may well reject the claim for a heart treatment later on, on the grounds of mis-declaration.

A word of warning here. There are many hybrid insurance cum investment schemes such as, Unit Linked Insurance Plan (ULIP), pension plans, etc. Life insurance is to taken for its core utility of insuring the life of the bread winner and not for any other purpose. If you want to invest your money, there are any number of investment options out there which will suit your purpose. So it maybe a good idea to delink investment from insurance and have your priorities in the right order.

RISK QUOTIENT

This is the amount of risk that you can comfortably take in your investments. Once you are aware of your risk quotient, you also know what sort of investments you can park your funds in.

We start by dividing the investments into three categories I, II, & III.

Category I investments

These have the minimum amount of risk. Although these are safe investments, it follows that the returns on these investments are dismal. Of these only two investment stand out in that they offer a better rate of interest than others. They are PPF and post office deposits.

Whereas the rate of interest on bank deposits and government securities will be in the range band of 0-7%, PPF and post office deposits offer 8% and above returns.

Thus even if you do invest in Category I investments, do ensure that the majority of these is in PPF and post office deposits. Of course there are some investments like Capital Gains bonds, tax saving bonds, etc., in which you may invest to avail some facility offered therein.

They include the following:

a. Bank deposits.

b. Government bonds and securities

c. Public provident fund

d. Post office deposits and financial instruments

e. Savings accounts

Then there is the liquidity factor. Liquidity indicates the period of time required to convert the investments into ready cash. In this regard it is the Bank deposits which really scores over the others. A bank deposit can generally be prematurely encashed within 48 hours. The only loss you will suffer is a deduction in the rate of return. The worst culprit in this regard is the government securities, which often has a lock-in period. Post office deposits usually require about fifteen days to be prematurely encashed.

Withdrawals from your PPF account can also be done within 48 hrs, but the amount is limited. As detailed in the section on PPF, you can withdraw upto amount you had in the account 4 years back or 50% of the amount 1 year back. This can actually be good for you, because it ensures that all your investments in PPF does not go up in smoke together.

Thus it is a good idea to have a certain percentage of your category I investments in the form of Bank deposits as they will offer you the liquidity that you will require to cope with unforeseen emergencies. In fact your total investments in each category can be spread in the various options available in order to achieve the most from your money with the least risk.

Category II investments

These investments come with a standard risk. Although they are not as safe as those in Category I, they are relatively safe and offer a higher return.

They include the following :

a. Gold and gold bonds

b. Debt funds (Mutual funds investing in debt instruments)

c. Gilt funds (Mutual funds investing in Gilt)

d. Company deposits of established companies including bonds, etc.

e. Insurance related schemes

Category III investments

These offer the maximum returns but carries the maximum amount of risk.

They include the following :

a. Company shares

b. Equity related mutual funds

c. Commodities and commodity funds

d. Deposits of companies offering a higher than market rate of interest

I would like to add here that I have not included property as an investment opportunity. This does not include the property we buy for our own residential use. This is a necessity. As discussed in detail earlier, any investment in real estate has a higher than nominal risk, mainly because India has not yet developed our real estate market. Much of the property in our country is mired in litigations of various sorts which may not be known or may not be revealed at the time of purchase. Again the number of unscrupulous real estate agents, property developers and brokers involved in this game makes it a potential minefield for the uninitiated buyer who may pay up without realising the pit falls involved. Compared to this sort of risk, the returns are not that attractive. Again property is not a liquid asset. When you need to sell it in a hurry, you will never get the market price and may well have to resort to a distress sale, well below the market price.

However someone who knows the rules of the game and is familiar with real estate as an investment tool can surely include this in his investment portfolio. The major advantage of any sort of property is that it is a tangible asset, where you will very seldom incur a capital loss. In other words during slack periods also property prices do not go down as much as the equity market, but during boom times it manages to keep pace with other investments.

SOME THUMB RULES FOR INVESTING

Having explained the various categories of investments, it is now easy to match the risk profile of the individual against the investments. But before any major and serious investment is concerned, certain points have to be kept in mind so that the investor does not end up losing his entire capital.

There a few thumb rules to be followed when doing this :

1. **The age of the individual:** In other words the older you are the less of your savings as a percentage should be in category III (risky) investments. A young man who has a lifetime of earnings and savings ahead of him can afford to put in upto 70% of his savings in equity related investments whereas a retired man cannot afford to put even a penny in equity because of the inherently high risk potential of equities.

2. **The disposable income of the individual:** As a general rule, the more the disposable income which can then be saved, the higher the risk that can be taken. An individual who can save only 10% of his earnings must make sure that he guards this amount against untoward risk. On the other hand a person earning a high salary and able to save more than 50% of his savings can take a calculated risk and put a higher proportion of his savings in a riskier investment such as equity.

3. **The time period that the money can remain invested:** Generally the longer the time period, the more the risk can be taken in the hope that in the longer term the risk will average out. But if the amount invested is required in a short interval of say, less than a year, it is always better to keep the money in a bank deposit. History has shown that investment in a high risk instrument like equity shares has given the maximum returns over a period of 10 years or more, provided the company has been well chosen.

4. **The job profile of the individual :** If the investor is not sure whether he will be in the same type of job, earning the same salary for the next few years, he cannot afford to risk his savings in a risky investment. But if the investor is in a good job and his job security is assured, then he can definitely afford to take a higher risk on his investment in the hope of a higher return.

The above factors will assist the individual in determining his risk profile, i.e., the amount of risk that he can take. The stock market is the riskiest investment avenue, but comes with the largest potential for gain. Thus a young individual with no major commitments and a steady job can invest a major portion of his disposable income on equities, but a retired person cannot afford to take any risk with his retirement benefits and must stay away from equities.

Thus it is necessary for every individual to know his risk profile before investing the hard earned money. Once you know the amount of risk you can take, you can select the most suitable investment instrument in that category and invest.

TAX PLANNING

Tax planning is an important tool in order to get the most from your salary. It is best to start the tax planning for the year from the beginning of the financial year, i.e., from April onwards. This will give you enough time to choose the best instrument that fits your profile from the many options available. Delaying the tax planning will make you resort to last minute decisions which often will prove to tbe the wrong choice in the long-term.

There are many tax exemptions available under different sections of the Income Tax Act and it is advisable to know these well in order to take advantage of the exemptions. Some of them are as listed below.

Sec 80C: Investments in instruments covered under this section can be deducted from your taxable income upto a maximum limit of Rs 100000. They include Public Provident Fund (PPF), Employee Provident Fund (EPF), Equity Linked Savings Scheme (ELSS), National Savings Certificate (NSC), Life Insurance and ULIP premiums, approved pension plans and principal amount of home loans.

Sec 80D: Premiums paid for mediclaim and health insurance is covered under section 80D can be exempted from the taxable income upto a maximum limit of Rs 15000. This limit is increased to Rs 20,000/- for senior citizens.

Sec 80DD: In case of a dependant family member with sever disability an amount of Rs 50000 is permitted to be deducted from the taxable income, provided this amount is spent on the treatment and is supported by bills, etc.

Sec 80E: Section 80E gives tax exemption on education loans taken for higher studies in India and abroad.

Sec 80G: Under section 80G, donations to approved charitable institutions and funds are eligible for tax exemption subject to a maximum limit of 10% of your gross total income.

Sec 24 : Repayment of a housing loan upto a maximum limit of Rs 1.5 lakh is permitted to be deducted from the taxable income. This section covers only the interest component of the loan repayment. Joint borrowers can avail of total tax exemption of Rs 3 lakh.

Once you are aware of the above tax exemptions allowed, it is easy to look for various schemes which provide such exemptions and invest accordingly in order to get the maximum benefit and reduce your tax outflow. This should be a continuous effort and not left to the last few days of the financial year.

THE DIRECT TAX CODE

Recently the Finance Ministry has brought out the discussion paper on the Direct Tax Code (DTC). The initial paper invited howls of protest from the interested stakeholders which resulted in a revised paper on DTC being brought out. These proposals are expected to be brought into force from the next financial year, i.e., April 2011.

The following are the important features of the revised DTC.

Housing

The new proposal aims to do away with taxing of any property not let out or self occupied and should bring relief to those who have a second property and are unable to rent it out for various reasons. However loans on such property will not be entitled to any deduction under Section 24. Such deduction will continue on loans for self occupied house upto a maximum limit of Rs 1.5 lakh.

Insurance

Existing exemptions are retained but only for pure insurance plans. The ministry is expected to shortly bring out clarification on which life insurance schemes qualify for such exemptions. Currently maturity proceedings of life insurance plans are exempted from tax under the EEE (exempt, exempt, exempt) regime, i.e., tax rebate on investing, tax benefits on gains made by the fund and accumulating to the benefit of the investor and tax exemption on maturity value. This is expected to continue but for pure life insurance policies only.

Other insurance products such as ULIP, etc., will come under EET (Exempt, Exempt, Tax). This means that the maturity proceeds of the scheme will come under the tax net.

Annuity proceeds will enjoy the EEE benefits and will encourage long-term investments which will lead to a better retired life for the individuals.

Equity

The worst blow to the investor will be under the new capital gains tax which is expected to come into force under the revised DTC. Whereas earlier, all profits accruing from shares retained for longer than one year was fully exempted from capital gains tax, this is set to change from the next financial year. Under the DTC, capital gains for profits made from the sale of shares will come under the tax net. But relief will be provided as the entire profits will not be taxable, instead a certain percentage to be decided after further discussions will be taxable and added to the taxable income.

Mutual Funds

Under the DTC the exemption allowed under section 80C is expected to be raised to Rs 3 lakh from the present Rs 1 lakh for various investments including mutual funds (ELSS). Further whereas earlier only equity funds were covered under this section, debt oriented funds will also be included under the revised proposals.

Long-term capital gains tax will be calculated at applicable rates to be announced and added to the taxable income of the investor. However to avail of 'long-term' status the units will have to be held for more than one year from the end of the financial year in which it is purchased.

However, it is important to note that the DTC is still in the discussion stage and may be subject to further changes as required before it becomes applicable.

The end game

Investments made wisely will result in making your money grow. Thus it is necessary to take informed decisions and benefit from the advantages of the various investment opportunities. But remember to constantly monitor your investments and switch between them if the conditions so require. Those with substantial investments are advised to take the advice of professional analysts so that their investments give them better returns.

Happiness is not in the mere possession of money; it lies in the joy of achievement, in the thrill of creative effort.- Franklin D Roosevelt.

***

7
MAN MANAGEMENT

"If everyone is moving forward together, the success takes care of itself."
Henry Ford

Man management is perhaps the most relevant topic in today's world. It is a proven fact that a motivated team can do much more work in the allotted time than a team which is not. And this is where the art of man management begins. Whole series of books have been written on this topic alone. I have tried to put of it in a nutshell for easy reading.

Pundits differ in their view of man management. Some say it is an art, which is ingrained into individuals and can only be fine-tuned, never learnt afresh if you do not already have it in you. Others say it is a science, based on the study of human nature and can be mastered by anyone who cares to do so.

Whatever the truth, the fact is that man management is here to stay. In the good old days when HRD and PR where just words in the dictionary, people did not bother much about man management. Then what has changed that within a span of two decades that it has suddenly become so important?

Many things have changed for the better in the last few years. Employees, for one have become more educated, more informative and thus less prone to being bullied and exploited. Services have become less labour intensive and more intellect based where the input of the employee has an enhanced effect on the growth of the company. Again, due to the explosion of the media, both printed and television, employees are now more aware of their rights.

All this had made the handling of employees a very delicate and specialised job. Human Resource Development is that department that basically looks after man management and employee welfare. Today in almost all large companies there is a separate department for HRD. All companies take the subject of man management very seriously.

What I am in fact trying to get at is the importance and relevance of man management in today's scenario. Even in our day to day life the art of man management plays an extremely important role. Whether at home or in the office, with friends, neighbours or colleagues, a little bit of insight into man management can give long lasting rewards.

WHAT IS MAN MANAGEMENT?

Now that we know that man management is important and necessary, let us see what exactly it is. Is it a code of conduct, a set of rules, a practical formulation or what is it?

Very simply put, man management is the art of dealing with people. There are no rules, regulations, theories or any set formula. We are all born with the inbuilt knowledge of how to get along with others. The child, when most vulnerable, knows that a sweet smile and a lisp or two can make people do almost anything for them. This is the most basic form of man management - when an infant can make people dance to his tunes with a smile and a lisp. Similarly some people are more adept than others at handling people. With a little bit of effort it is possible for all of us to be able to get along with others and manage relationships with other people favourably.

Remember, man management is not only for company honchos and businessmen, it is useful for every individual whether in the office, at home or in the market place. It teaches us how to handle others effectively and sensitively to make a lasting and mutually satisfying relationship.

An important aspects of man management is to refine our own character. A man with good character, without petty biases and ill will towards others, who is straightforward and direct, at the same time humble and polite will find it easy to manage others. He does not need any degree or diploma in man management because he has already mastered the art of managing others through his own way of life. Human beings are essentially simple souls. They respect a person who can wield authority with panache without abusing it.

Honesty is an important personal traits essential in dealing with others. Lead by example and practice what you preach. Add to this a dash of fairness, a slice of discipline, a sprinkling of hard work and a dose of solid leadership and you have the recipe of a great leader, whether at work, with your friends or at home with your family.

In many places in this section I have used the word leader. That does not mean it only applies to senior managers and the like. Everyone is a team leader in his/her sphere of life, whether at the work station, at home or at play. Even juniors should consider themselves potential team leaders and start building on their man management capabilities. In fact it is the junior level management of today who are the movers and shakers of tomorrow. Thus they must make it a habit to polish their man management skills so that they can step into the shoes of their seniors without much trouble.

HOW TO BE A GOOD MAN MANAGER

Being a good man manager is not very tough. Most people have all the innate qualities for this, it just requires to be polished. A good man manager is successful in most fields of his job. Obviously how far he may rise in the organisation depends on other factors such as his qualifications, his hard work and determination, the results he produces and so on. But it is easier for a person with man management skills to rise to the top rather than someone who is not a good man manager. Below are a few points which will go a long way in honing your skills of man management.

Treat Everybody as Human Beings First

One of the principal fundamentals in dealing with people is to always keep in mind that others are also ordinary human beings. Every human has his own weaknesses which are known to him. Just as you make mistakes others too have the right to make mistakes. All humans have their own strengths, weaknesses, biases and vulnerabilities. We all have our good days and bad days. There are days when we get up feeling on top of the world and days when we know that whatever has to go wrong, will go wrong that day.

Just as we have these traits in us, others too have them. Thus it is difficult to predict the behaviour of others correctly at all times. A good man manager always makes allowances for others, mood swings and state of mind. For example one of the employees, who is generally good at his job and rarely makes a mistake makes a blunder. What do you do?

Your options are many. For one you can call him up and blast him. He might accept and keep quiet or he may answer back. The reaction of people to different situations is not always the same. Your raving and ranting may make him disheartened and demotivated. Remember, he is generally a good worker and good workers take offense to unnecessary disciplining more than recalcitrant ones. Thus they have to be handled more sensitively than others.

A second option for you is to ignore the whole issue as if it never happened. This may work for really good workers who discipline themselves and make their best effort to minimise their errors. Such people will own up their mistakes and will try their best not to repeat such mistakes. But if you ignore such mistakes it may send the wrong signals to the other employees. Some may take it as a sign of your weakness while others may think that they too are allowed to make such mistakes. Thus this option may have serious consequences.

The third and best option is to handle the whole episode with sensitivity. You have to remember that the person in front of you is as human as you are and susceptible to making mistakes. Thus you have to explain to him the consequences of his error and get from him a commitment that the same will not be repeated. This way you have sent out a clear message to everyone that you are monitoring them and will not hesitate to pull them up if required. At the same time, by handling it in a humane manner, you have diffused the situation and not allowed it to snowball into something more serious. Most humans when faced with this situation will readily accept their mistakes and provided you have played your cards right will get back to their work without feeling any rancour either towards you or the company.

Here I would like to emphasise upon three words - apathy, empathy and sympathy.

Apathy means lack of interest or enthusiasm. Your co-worker is explaining to you the health problems he and his wife are facing, instead of listening with involvement, you yawn, look at your watch or look at the door often. This is an apathetic attitude. People are quick to estimate your attitude to their tale of woe. The moment they sense that you are apathetic, most of them will just shut up and get out. You have then, lost the power to motivate, lost an opportunity to gain a good friend or even lost the respect you had earlier.

Sympathy, on the other hand is the sharing or agreeing with someone else's feelings. In the above scenario, the sympathetic attitude would be to listen to what the other person has to say, share his mental anguish and help him in whatever way you can.

But the best attitude that you can develop is empathy. Empathy is the power of imaginatively entering into and understanding the other person's feelings. An empathetic attitude will mean that you not only share, but also understand other person's problems or sorrow from the bottom of your heart. An empathetic attitude can reap rewards for you from your colleagues, friends, juniors or seniors. Thus you have to learn the art of empathy. When someone is narrating his problems, don't let your mind wander and think of whether you will be able to reach home tonight in time for the cricket match. Rather, put yourself in the situation that is being explained and try to live the scene. Once you learn to practice the empathetic attitude, it will come automatically and you will definitely be the better off for it.

Be disciplined and professional yourself

There is an old saying 'Respect is commanded, not demanded'. You may be a top guy in the office, the cash cow, so to say, the pivot around which your office activities revolve, but if you want to get the respect of your colleagues, you have to earn it. There is a difference between being a boss who is feared and one who is respected. And respect is one thing you cannot force from people. People may obey you, out of fear of losing their jobs, out of fear of being dressed down in front of their colleagues or to keep away from your nasty temper. But that is not respect.

Some people think being a boss gives them the license to be indisciplined while expecting discipline from their employees. This attitude is totally wrong. A boss who is himself disciplined has the moral authority to discipline others, whereas one who is himself indisciplined will find that he has lost the authority to discipline his juniors. A small example will illustrate this better. Say, you are a manager, with about twenty people working under you. If you dress soberly, come to office on time, do not take undue advantage of your position and deal with your colleagues and juniors pleasantly, people will respect you.

One of the dictionary meanings for the word 'professional' is 'extremely competent for a job'. We are all doing jobs at all times, whether in the office, at home or at play and thus being competent in these activities will make us better individuals. One of the best complements I ever received is 'You are a true professional'. If you have a professional attitude towards life, you will find people gravitating towards you, simply because you are good at what you do and the world admires competent people. So take every job seriously and try to complete it in the time frame that you have slotted for it. Be answerable to yourself. There's an old saying that a successful man is always answerable to himself first and to others later. Be you own worst critic and you will find very few people will criticise you.

Being a true professional takes a lot of effort than is apparent. You have to be competent, disciplined, time bound, courteous, empathetic to others, at the same time demanding and firm. Then you will not only excel in whatever you are doing, but you will earn the respect and admiration of all.

Do not backbite

Talking behind someone's back is one of the easiest traps you can fall into, simply because that person is not there to defend himself. It is very easy to criticise, but the fact is that by overly criticising someone else you are exposing our own insecurities. In general do not say anything about someone which you cannot say on his face. Many times you will find people instigating you directly or indirectly to say something adverse about others. Don't fall into this trap. Even if you do, always make a leeway for his wrong action, by giving an excuse for it. For example, if one of your colleagues has a habit of consistently coming late, and you happen to discuss this with others, you can add that 'actually since he is coming through congested localities, the traffic may be delaying him'.

This does not of course mean that you will ignore and condone such activities of your juniors. If one of your juniors habitually comes late for work, you have to face him squarely and make him understand that this sort of attitude will not do. Before launching into a tirade against the poor fellow, find out why he is coming late everyday. Maybe he has a genuine problem, which you can set right. But talking about it behind his back is not going to help at all. There are many situations where you have to bell the cat. These situations have to be faced and not avoided.

In fact you can reverse this habit. Instead of backbiting, start praising others behind their back. This has a double effect. The person hearing this will brush up his own act, in order to be praised by you in front of others. Again the person whom you are praising will definitely get to hear about it from someone or the other and improve himself in order to be worthy of your praise.

I have often used this trick to advantage in order to improve my juniors. There was this guy who used to invariably leave early in order to beat the office rush. I had already spoken to him about this, but he continued with this habit. In fact even an indirect threat of losing his job had no effect. He was actually a good worker and I did not want to lose him. Finally I hit upon this idea of reverse backbiting as I call it. Next time he left, I made it a point to talk to those colleagues of his, who I knew where close to him. I let out the fact that although he was leaving early, he would make sure to finish whatever work he had in hand before leaving his table. I continued this for a week and soon enough observed him working harder in the afternoons to complete his work for the day. Finally he was cured of the habit of leaving early.

Praise in public, discipline behind closed doors

Never underestimate the power of a well-deserved praise tactfully said in public. The good will generated by such public praise will reap rich rewards for you in future. Everybody has a high sense of self worth and self respect. By acknowledging the good work and contribution of an employee or a junior in public, his status in the eyes of his peers will increase and so will his self respect. This will undoubtedly increase his effort and output in future. But there is a catch - Don't overdo it. It is easy to catch on to an undeserved praise and you wouldn't want to be sycophantic. Thus if a praise is in order, do not hesitate to give it - in front of others!! The value of it will be then multiplied in the eyes of the receiver.

On the other hand, if you have to admonish or pull up an employee, never do it in public. Remember everybody has an ego and if the ego is hurt, people will retaliate. If you push people to the wall, they will fight. Never corner someone with no chance of an escape route. If an employee has made a serious mistake, approach him in private and put the facts before him and ask for his explanation. If an employee acknowledges his mistake, is apologetic and promises to do better, accept his apology in good faith, tell him how to avoid such errors in future and move on. There is no point in rubbing it in once the mistake has been accepted.

If a person does not accept his mistake and insists that he has done no wrong, don't push it. Pushing the point will only mean that you are trying to prove him to be a liar. In such a scenario, tell him that he may have committed the mistake without realising it. Explain to him that we are all humans, that it is human nature to make mistakes, but you have to learn from each mistake so as not to repeat them in future. Still if he is adamant and denies any wrong doing, give him the benefit of doubt and close the matter. But keep an eye on such an employee and his work.

If an employee repeats such mistakes and steadfastly denies them every time, then it is time for a showdown. Such a person can be dangerous to the well being of the organisation and needs to be disciplined. Such disciplining should be done in stages. There is no point in flying off the handle and blasting the poor fellow. This will demoralize the entire team with disastrous results. The first step is to have a private chat with the offender. The second step is to have a meeting with his colleagues and department heads where he is told to put in a better performance. If he does not improve, a show-cause notice can be issued. Usually before this stage most employees will realise their mistake and pull up their act. However if the employee does not improve and continues to make serious mistakes, then it is time to bid him good bye.

Inculcate team work and team spirit:

One of the most important pillars of an efficient organisation is teamwork. Every organisation is like a machine. Every part of the machine is important and contributes to the proper functioning. Similarly every person in the organisation is an important and essential member of the team. By inculcating team spirit and promoting team work the entire organisation can be made to work like a well oiled and an efficient machine.

How do you inculcate team spirit? The most important word here is you. Collective responsibility, collective pride and collective gains are the drivers to a good team. Every cog in the wheel is important, no matter how small. The most important factor in this is that the senior members of the team must give credit where it is due and sometimes even when it is not particularly due to the juniors down the line. When something goes wrong the senior members must have the confidence and the strength to stand up and be held responsible for it instead of passing the buck. It is very easy to blame for the failure on some junior members of the team, but once you do it, you have lost the respect and goodwill of the team for ever and the team will never function as efficiently again. On the other hand, if as a senior member you take the responsibility and shield the juniors down the line, you have their respect and support for all times to come.

GOOD COMMUNICATION BRINGS BENEFITS

Communication is one of the most important factors in good team work. Generally you are used to top-down communication, i.e. the seniors tell the junior members what is to be done and the juniors are expected to do it. I have attended many management meetings where the boss does all the talking, assisted once in a while by his senior managers. There is simply no horizontal communication. In fact you have to go one step further and promote bottom-up communication. That happens when the junior members are free to stand up and give their ideas without fear of being ridiculed or targeted. In fact many management studies have proved that some of the brightest, most revolutionary and successful ideas come from the bottom of the pyramid. The younger members of the team are fresh and have an unbiased view of the whole situation. They must always be encouraged to speak up and their ideas given due weightage.

Remember it takes a lot of courage and conviction for a junior to stand up and speak out his ideas. We are all captives of our hidden fears and insecurities. Thus if someone down the line speaks up, it tells volumes about the strength of his character. He should first be appreciated for coming out with the idea and it should be discussed with due seriousness without the smirks and snide comments which generally follow when a junior comes out with a genuine idea. Once the idea is given due thought it does not matter whether it is ultimately accepted or rejected. The fact that the seniors have appreciated and discussed the point raised by him is by itself enough to give a boost to the junior's confidence. On the other hand, if his ideas are ignored or made fun of, then he will probably never speak up again and you have lost the services of a bright young brain.

Therefore in every meeting seniors must encourage their juniors to speak up and come out with what is on their mind. Then only will the organisation have the vibrancy and energy which comes with youth. The senior members are victims of their experiences, biases and rigid thinking. If this is not diluted by the open mindedness of the younger members, the organisation will not go forward at the speed that is necessary to take it forward.

REWARD GOOD WORKERS

What most management gurus and big organisations miss out on is the power of reward. Reward need not be monetary. It may be in the form of instituting an award to the most useful member of the team, the member with the brightest ideas, the most punctual member, etc. A reward or award system brings out the best in any person because it gives them recognition. If I work better than my colleague, get better results, am the one to be called upon in times of crisis, is looked upon to give ideas in the meetings and is the one on whose table the toughest projects land, then it is only natural that I expect something more from the organisation. The easiest way to kill initiative is to treat all employees as equals no matter what their output. The time will come when the ones who are more efficient and more competent will get fed up and look for other openings or tone down their effort, if they are not compensated for it.

A friend of mine in the service industry took this idea of mine seriously enough to start with an award system for three categories. Firstly for the employee who was rarely absent and always punctual, secondly for the person who customers looked out for and approached freely and thirdly for the person who had the best interaction in their daily meetings. He was amazed by the turnaround in the attitude of many of his employees. People who had earlier been moribund and sedentary started being energetic and taking an active interest in the meetings and in the customers. So much so that finally my friend introduced further three categories of awards and to this day he has not regretted the decision.

The power of recognition is huge. We all want to be recognised in life. If at the end of the year the management singles out the best employees and awards them for their dedication and sincerity, then they feel that they have got a just return for all the hard work that they have put in. Again, they realise that these characteristics are important for the organisation and so they start putting in more effort. Unfortunately most top level companies have no such systems in place. Even promotions are on seniority basis. This is invariably the best way to kill individualism and get the best people out of the company once they realise where they stand in terms of seniority.

GOOD WORKERS ARE THE FIRST TO RECOGNISE BAD MANAGEMENT

It is fact that most good workers are bad at bargaining and sycophancy. They think that their work speaks volumes of their worth in the company. Thus if they do not get a raise, a promotion or due recognition, they are unlikely to go to the top management for addressing their problem. They would rather continue working, but bitter feeling against the management starts building up. There are two logical endings to this scenario. Their performance level dips due to lack of motivation and they too become part of the faceless crowd of average workers who work just enough to keep their jobs. But others who are more ambitious and adventurous will definitely start looking around for a better opening elsewhere. The fact is that such good workers do not have to look too hard for a change. Word gets around, head hunters get into the act and before long the good employee who had been neglected by the employers has been absorbed by another company!

In such cases, the loss is of the organisation. Many senior management people in top level companies are of the opinion that when an employee leaves the organisation, the loss is his. They feel that they can always get another guy in his place. This is a wrong concept. The departure of a good employee is always the loss of the organisation.

A buzzword in management circles these days is 'attrition rate'. This is an indication of how long people stay with the organisation. Companies with high attrition blame the employees for running away. But do they look within their own organisation to find the root of the problem? Invariably no! When you talk of a company with a high attrition rate, it indicates a serious malaise within the organisation which needs to be addressed immediately. When employees do not want to stay for more than a few months or a couple of years, it indicates bad man management skills on the part of the organisation.

Then there is something called the attrition rate of the industry. It is the level of the employee loyalty within the industry as a whole. The software industry has a high attrition rate. This indicates that within this industry employees tend to change companies faster. There is no point in blaming the industry for this. The fact is that in this sunrise industry there are too many new players who have entered to make a fast buck. Naturally employee welfare is not at the top of their list, making more and more profits is. If the software industry as a whole has a high attrition rate, how come front line companies have a low attrition rate? The answer is simple – they care for their employees and have in place a system for the welfare of their employees.

Once again the people who leave the company will be the good ones. And the way to hold them back is simply to reward their good work.

Be fair and without bias:

Fairness is a very important virtue in an individual, especially for someone who is a team leader. To be fair means to be free from any sort of discrimination. Most of us come with a set of biases and prejudices. As a result of our background, upbringing and experiences, most of the decisions we make are invariably coloured with our own likes and dislikes. This is known as having a bias.

This has an important bearing on man management. The employees are quick to know whether or not the boss is prejudiced against them in any way or the other. As a team leader your job is to take the team along with you and get the best out of them. For this it is necessary to treat every person equally on his merit alone. The moment you have a biased opinion about someone, your behaviour towards the person will undergo a subtle change which will be noticeable by him. This will have the effect of demotivating the person, for he thinks that no matter what effort he puts in you will always be against him.

Thus it is necessary to clear your mind and look at every person as an individual, not on the basis of his colour, creed, background, nationality, etc. This can be used to good effect with a bit of effort. If you make an effort to be fair and succeed in dealing honestly and fairly with your juniors, you will build up a reservoir of good will which will show in the effort put in by your team members.

Being fair is a very important virtue. If you deal with people in a straightforward manner nine times out of ten, they will reciprocate with respect and honour. Of course you may get the odd bad egg, who has to be dealt with immediately and firmly. But on the whole a fair team leader invariably has the respect of his juniors all along the line.

Honesty is the best policy

In every sphere of life an honest, straightforward and truthful man stands out like a beacon. In today's scenario it may be unfashionable, but at the bottom of our hearts we know that we like respect and gravitate towards an honest man. Honesty is a great virtue in all individuals and we should work towards it. In man management it assumes special significance since if a team member is seen as being honest and truthful the team leaders will respect him for it and take his command to heart.

On the contrary a dishonest team leader evokes revulsion and hatred in the minds of the juniors. They do not know whether he is being honest or not. So they do not give him credit even when he deserves it. They may go along with him and continue doing a good job, but that extra effort will definitely be missing. If the boss is perceived as being a cheat, then it is easier for people down the line to resort to dishonest methods for their own benefit. Thus the organisation starts bleeding internally and if not checked will lead to an early death.

Unfortunately in today's industry honesty is at a premium. Profits, turnover, etc., are the buzzwords in a capitalist society where honesty and truthfulness are not exactly seen as virtues. But this is only in the short term. In the long run people with these important traits stand out and are recognised for what they are. It is easy to be dishonest in small matters. Soon you will find that lying has become second nature and soon enough you will be trapped in the web of lies and deceit of your own making. It is never too late to break free of all this and lead a life of dignity where you are known as an honest man.

If you look at our industries this truism stands out. The industry leaders you really respect are those whose personal credentials are above board. Those industrialists who take the shortcut invariably fall by the wayside sooner than later. It is those who run their business with pride and integrity that reap the real benefits. The finest example is Bill Gates. Perhaps the most successful industrialist of our times, he has an impeccable personal record. His employees are happy with him, because he rewards them for their labour. His share holders are happy with him because he distributes his profits to them. The Government is happy with him because he does not evade taxes and is an ambassador of the country. And he is a philanthropist who helps charitable institutions.

"I hope I shall always have firmness and virtue enough to maintain, what I consider the most enviable of all titles, the character of an honest man'"

– George Washington

Humility pays

One of the best qualities in a man is humility. A man with humility stands out in the crowd of egoistic pushers. Humility is all about overcoming our personal ego and thinking about the person in front of us as an equal.

Life is a cycle. Sometimes you are on top and sometimes you may find yourself right at the bottom. What people often forget is that when they are on top, it is but a temporary phase. One half turn of the wheel and they find themselves at the bottom.

Thus when you are right on top, you should be humble in the knowledge that it may not take too long for you to hit the bottom. Similarly, someone at the bottom must have confidence that one day the wheel will turn and take him to the top.

A few tips to be humble. Drop the 'I' from your conversation. A person who uses the 'I' word often comes across as an egoistic one.

Try using 'We'. You will find that people respond better to this. If the 'I' stands up it forms a barrier between people. Make the 'I' lie down and it becomes a bridge between individuals where earlier barriers existed.

Forget the blame culture

Everybody is familiar with an overbearing boss who looks for scapegoats and starts blaming everybody but himself when the going gets rough. Blaming someone else unnecessarily is an exercise in futility which has no gains but has many disadvantages. If the employee is indeed responsible, it is always better to take him aside and have a quiet but firm word with him. Give him a warning that such mistakes will not be overlooked in future and let him know that you will be watching him. Blaming someone brings down the morale of the team as the team initiative will be reduced as each one tries to cover himself in order to avoid the blame should things go wrong. Similarly if a colleague is responsible for any mistakes, there is no point in blaming him. The first action is to tell him to rectify the fault. He can then be told where his mistakes lie and ask him to avoid such mistakes in future. This way an unhealthy situation can be avoided, the morale of the team is not affected and the concerned person is made aware of the errors in his way of working.

Some people look the other way when a mistake has been committed and try to rectify it themselves. This is a wrong procedure and the employee will continue making such mistakes. Every person should be told to correct his own mistakes in order to avoid repetition and a chance must be given to him to prove himself. This way people will continue to improve their skills and learn from their mistakes.

DISCOURAGE SYCOPHANCY

In any organisation there are bound to be some people whose main aim in life is to flatter and misguide their superiors for their own petty ends. Such people are to be kept at arm's length as they sow the seeds of discontent and demotivate others. Unfortunately most of us have a weakness for flattery in any form and often give undeserved importance to the flatterer. Such an attitude will make the real workers disheartened and their output will invariably deteriorate. The good workers usually do not need to resort to sycophancy in order to flourish on the job. This sort of behaviour is usually resorted to by those in the organisation who are not good in their job and thus suffer from a feeling of insecurity. They thus cosy up to their bosses and make up for their lack of performance by flattery.

Small things matter

It is the small thoughtful gestures that will give big rewards in man management. For example, remember the birth dates of your colleagues and make it a point to wish them in the morning. Again, share their joys and sorrows wholeheartedly, because anyone can differentiate between genuine feelings and superficial ones. If one of your colleagues is unwell, send him a get well soon card and pay him a visit. Enquire after the health of the near and dear ones of your friends and colleagues. It is these small things that go a long way in fostering a feeling of team spirit and bonhomie and make you a good man manager.

Add atouch of humour

Sometimes it may happen that the pressure on all the employees builds up and they are unable to perform to their full abilities, because of the tension prevailing all around. Thus when the going gets tough the leader must not fall prey to the pressure and get unduly tensed up. Don't forget that tension also, like humour is contagious. It does not take too long for the tension emanating from the boss's office to spread all over. People end up scared to take decisions for the fear of being reprimanded. Where a smile or a good word would have worked wonders, frowns and blame games undermine individual performance and leads to more errors and delays.

Do what you say

Place a premium on what you promise. When you give an appointment make sure to keep it. When you promise to help someone in need, make good on your promise. When you tell someone that you will call back, be sure to call back in time. Same goes for mails. In short, once you have committed to an action, be sure to deliver it. That will differentiate you from the crowd and people will learn to trust you and depend on you.

And say what you do

Many people do something and say something else. Thus in general there is no value for the words of such people. The best course of action would be to state clearly what you are going to do. In other words make your actions clear and transparent. For example, if you are going to give an adverse report on your junior, say so and do it in a transparent manner. The person who is sweet on the outside, but reports against a junior secretly, soon loses the respect of his junior. Thus saying what you are going to do and then doing it will ensure that people respect and trust your words.

TEAM BUILDING

Team building is like a game. Human nature and responses are more often than not predictable. Thus you are more or less aware of the other person's reactions to your actions. If you spare a thought for the reactions before you act, it will be a lot easier for you to act in a manner that it will not boomerang on you. Whether you are a team leader or a team member, remember the chain is only as good as the weakest link. Thus you have to do your work properly if the team is to be a success. No member of a team can relax and hope that the other members will carry them along. Thus an important aspect of team work is individual performance. Some members of the team may be sanguine in the belief that the other, more dynamic members of their team will make up for their lack of ability. But the fact is that if even a few members of the team do not perform, the performance of the team as a whole goes down. Thus each and every member of the team must put in their best effort if the team is to succeed as a whole.

Another important aspect is mutual respect. No team can function effectively if members do not respect each other. Every team member young or old has something to offer or he would not be in the team in the first place. Thus it is the job of the leader to find the best role for each member of the team. Team leaders must hold frequent brain storming sessions where everybody expresses their views and are heard by the others. Not only will this boost their confidence, the ideas put forth by the young members often prove to be quite useful. It often occurs that during such brain storming sessions, the views of the younger members of the team are rejected out of hand and even scoffed at. This is a dangerous attitude and will result in the young members clamping up altogether, resulting in a loss for the team in general. Thus all team members must be encouraged to come out with their ideas and views at all times.

BRAINSTORMING

Brainstorming is a process which has been used extensively across industries in areas where innovative alternatives must be found. It is best done in small groups led by a recorder who simply lists every idea that is offered by any member of the group. There are some simple ideas for working creatively in groups. Brainstorming is extremely useful as the divide between seniors and juniors is usually sharp and in usual circumstances juniors prefer to lie low. Brainstorming is the ideal tool to make them open up and offer their views and ideas freely without hesitation.

The key to successful brainstorming is to withhold criticism until the group has exhausted its creativity. Criticism can be very difficult to resist, especially when juniors brainstorm with seniors, because many of the ideas juniors provide will have technical flaws, and the ideas seniors provide may not be fully understood by the juniors, or may not be practical enough. But criticism at this point will kill creativity. In order to avoid the embarrassment of being criticised in front of a group, people will simply keep their ideas to themselves. It must be stressed before the brainstorming begins that there shall be no criticism, of ideas put forward by the juniors and in case of any such undue criticism, it must be quickly stopped and the prohibition on negative criticism enforced, or the brainstorming effort will be a waste of time. Needless to say constructive criticism is a tool for strengthening the system and should not be prohibited.

Encouraging all participants to freely offer solutions achieves many ends: it can allay fears that possible solutions have been overlooked; provide the insight of a fresh perspective to an expert; force the examination of good ideas that have powerful foes; or allow interesting, but ultimately unsuitable ideas to be raised and rejected in an equitable and public manner. After the brainstorming, participants should eliminate redundant ideas, and then use preliminary screening criteria to reduce the number of alternatives. The remaining alternatives can then be organised if that serves a purpose.

ADVANTAGES OF BRAINSTORMING

Team leaders must develop the habit of conducting brainstorming sessions whenever required. The advantages of brainstorming sessions are as follows :

1. Throws new solutions to problems. Juniors often view problems from different angles and come up with solutions which may have missed the seniors.

2. Develops good team spirit amongst the members of the team which will stand in good stead during crisis, periods of extra work load, etc.

3. Motivates all members of the team. When motivation levels are high the performance of each individual improves and life becomes a lot more efficient and organised.

4. Increases situational awareness of all the members as each member is forced to think on his own and suggest new ideas and solutions.

5. Improves leadership qualities in the senior management as they have to take the lead in the brainstorming session and show the way for the juniors to follow.

The team members must communicate effectively among themselves. No matter what the situation, if there is communication within the team, the problems can be discussed and finally sorted out. All members must make an effort at communicating with each other. Do not expect wonders from the other team members. Often we judge others by our own standards. This is detrimental to the development of the organisation as a whole and therefore judgement should be reserved until the facts and circumstances of the case are understood. Good communication among members will ensure free flow of ideas and result in an overall improvement in the output of the team. The team leader must take personal interest in improving communication.

Finally, all team members must have a collective sense of responsibility towards the team and towards achieving the ultimate goal. Every team member must take responsibility for the actions of the team and not indulge in the blame game should things go wrong. If mistakes are accepted and forgiven, the team can learn from them and move ahead.

PERSONAL QUALITY

It is well recognised across the industries that human output can be considerably enhanced by paying close attention to human attitudes, behaviour, expectations, demands, etc. One such quantitative yardstick in this is called personal quality. It has been established that by increasing the personal quality of their employees, corporates can expect an increased performance from them.

Manager International (TMI) defines personal quality as 'meeting other people's and one's own "bottomline" and "beyond bottomline" demands and expectations'. Bottomline quality has been defined as 'meeting concrete demands and expectations, e.g., time, quantity, finances, defect rate, durability, safety and guarantee.

Beyond bottomline, quality has been defined as meeting emotional expectations and desires, e.g., attitudes, commitment, behaviour, attention, credibility, consistency and loyalty.

How can the personal quality of an individual be judged? Here another term has been introduced known as 'Actual Performance' (AP). This is the quality of your present performance influenced in equal measure by what you expect of yourself and what the others expect and demand from you. The gap between the two is the indicator of how you can improve your personal quality.

Your self worth and attitude towards yourself influences your attitude towards others and life in general. A positive attitude and a confident personality helps you to feel good about yourself and increases self esteem.

This has a direct co-relation to what others think of you and your output in your workplace.

Thus hard work and effort increases your personal quality which in turn boost your self esteem and what others think about you.

POINTS TO PONDER :

1. In today's workplace every employee expects dignity and respect. Hence the concept of HRD (Human resource Development) and PR (Public Relation) assumes importance as every company tries to get the most of their employees by making them feel as part of the organisation, by understanding the needs of the employees and so on.

2. One of the first prerequisites to be a good man manager is to understand that all employees are humans first and employees later. The employer might have bought their skill, knowledge and time but not their souls. If managers think about this aspect, half the problems between employees and management will be solved.

3. A good manager must himself be disciplined and a professional, before he can hope to earn the respect of his juniors and co-workers. In this context it is important to note that respect must be commanded, not demanded.

4. In the office atmosphere back biting is a plague which eats at the innards of the organisation. Back biting should not be indulged in, especially by the senior people as word gets around and it can have a demoralising effect on the juniors.

5. The policy of praise in public, criticism in private goes a long way in improving the self confidence of the employee. Praise in public does immense good to the image of the employee, while quiet criticism within the four walls can make him realise his faults and prove effective in avoiding repetitions of the same.

6. Honesty and humility are two very important traits in a team leader. An honest man is always looked up to and a humble person is well liked and respected.

7. Blame culture should be abolished from the dictionary of corporates as no meaningful growth is possible in an organisation which thrives on the blame culture. This leads to avoidable situations like sycophancy, backbiting, etc. Hence the organisation itself must not condone any sort of blame culture since blaming is not the solution. The real solution is trying to make the employee realise his faults and correct them accordingly.

8. Do what you say and say what you do is one of the important by-words in ISO 9000 terminology. The concept can be borrowed for day-to day use and the client, employees, etc., feel that they are not being cheated,
9. Team building is extremely important in day to day management and must be encouraged in all its aspects. Team building ensures that all members of the team remain as one cohesive unit working for the continuous upliftment of the organisation.
10. Personal quality is an important HR tool in the current scenario and all employees must know and appreciate the values of personal quality.

***

8
CHARACTER MANAGEMENT

> *"Character cannot be developed in ease and quiet. Only through experience of trial and suffering can the soul be strengthened, ambition inspired, and success achieved. "*
>
> *– Helen Keller*

Character management is an old fashioned word these days. Nobody likes to talk about this subject. Today's children are never in mood to listen to moralistic lectures or even well meant advice from their parents and seniors. Parents are reluctant to confront their children and thus skip their duty of refining their children's character. They feel that schools should do the job. Schools today are so busy with their academic curriculum that they hardly have time for anything else. And schools do not want to take up the difficult and thankless job of character management for the fear of alienating the students. In short, the importance of character management has reduced over the years. In this materialistic world it does not matter what character a person has, as long as he is wealthy.

We have several excellent centres of education in our country which maintain high quality. Students passing out from these institutes become leaders in their chosen fields. However, the worst colleges and institutes come to the limelight, due to the misdeeds of a few of their students. Thus indiscipline is like cancer which must be banished at the first sign. Management of colleges and professional institutes must show that they have the nerve to tackle any sort of student backlash. Only then will the trouble makers lie low and allow the more serious students to pursue their studies.

The whole process of character formation starts from infancy. When a child throws his first tantrum, he is in effect sending out the first feeler which will decide his future behaviour. If the parent indulges him the first time and gives him the object of his tantrum the battle is half lost. Right from infancy children must be taught that there are certain limits to their behaviour. Parents should shoulder the entire responsibility of bringing up children in the correct manner. Many parents tend to shrug off from responsibility by blaming the schools, the child's friends, even indulgent grand parents for the bad behaviour of their children. I firmly believe that parents should have the courage to face up to the child as he grows and make him understand the priorities in life. Children are very adaptive and sensible. They are quick to learn and even quicker to push the limits of their parents indulgence.

Having said this, I must add that teachers in school also share responsibility in the child's upbringing. Many teachers today are of the opinion that their sole job is to teach the syllabus and nothing more. But they fail to understand that life itself is one big education and they are uniquely positioned to mould the child into a good student who will be a useful citizen in future.

Even some of the highly educated faculty in the professional colleges today shrug off this responsibility. If the faculty themselves are professional they will find that the students also respect them. Punctuality, time management, knowledge of the subject matter, fairness and the overall attitude of the faculty often goes a long way in moulding the students.

This is the reason why I have included this important topic in the book. Since this topic is shelved by the mentors, it would be worthwhile to devote a few pages to it here. The purpose is to emphasise the importance of character management and to suggest ways and means of improving our character so that we learn to live a fulsome life, be at peace with ourselves and the world around us. We can thus be a useful member of our society and contribute to it in more ways than one.

CHARACTER - YOUR SIGNATURE IN LIFE

Character is the signature of every individual. We are known by our character. In Japan, big corporate honchos commit suicide if there is a blemish on their character. Today we are such a materialistic society that if a person is wealthy, his character is overlooked.

The saddest part is that every time some straightforward politician or bureaucrat tries to bring in some legislation to prevent these criminals from contesting election, they are simply voted out or thrown out. That is the tragedy of a diverse democracy such as ours. We all know the uphill task the ex Election Commissioner T. N. Seshan had, to bring some sort of electoral reform so that the elections are a free and fair one. Today he is forgotten, and the wrong people continue to enjoy the privileges of power.

NEED TO FOCUS ON DEVELOPING THE CHARACTER

Character formation and character building was never on the agenda of either our policy makers or our intelligentsia. Our schools which earlier on had a subject called moral science have now turned away from trying to build the character of their wards. The schools feel that this is the job of the parents. Their job begins and ends with the academic part of education.

Either they do not know or do not want to know that education is just one part of the overall makeup of a person.

Parents on the other hand are quite comfortable with the academic routines dished out by the schools. Most parents fight shy of even trying to bring up the topic of character building with their children. Somewhere along the way, the character of the child has lost its relevance in the mad rush to get admissions to reputed schools, colleges, etc. Very few parents have the wish to see their children grow up as good human beings and useful citizens of the country. They are content to see their children become good money spinners rather than good human beings. They do not realise that money notwithstanding a person of good moral character towers above the others.

But life has a great way of evening out. The same children grow up to be immature adults. Many of them fail in their jobs and find it difficult to cope with the pressures of today's living. Their family life is more often than not in shambles. Naturally, a person who was not brought up in the right way does not know the meaning of the word sacrifice, compromise, tolerance, trust and truthfulness which are pillars of any successful relationship. Thus we hear of the ever increasing cases of divorce and break ups. People have no respect for each other. In other words, our society as a whole has started to slip. If we do not take note of this and take corrective actions it may not be too long before we end up becoming a decadent society with no moral values and only Mammon as our idol!

In such a scenario it is sensible to look back and see what our forefathers had to say about character management. Yes, our great religious leaders of yesteryears and philosophers of the bygone era did consider character to be an all important trait.

Most of the religious scriptures had strong advice to their followers about the way they should lead their lives in order to achieve their goal. They call it by different names, but all these scriptures give lessons on morality. It is time we looked back and relearnt these important lessons.

THE ORIGINAL SINS TO BE AVOIDED

The cardinal sins are pride, covetousness, lust, greed, anger, sloth and envy. All the scriptures more or less agreed that these are the vices which man has to avoid in order to attain salvation. Let us understand the meaning of these sins.

Pride

Pride is the first cardinal sins. Pride can be termed as the source from which other sins arise. It is a flaw in the nature of humans. Every human has it to a certain degree, but the desire to be more important than others, thinking of others as less worthy individuals than us, an unnatural joy in ones own position, failing to give deserving compliments to others, taking pleasure in the fact that we are more attractive than others are all signs of pride. There is an old saying "*Pride goes before a fall*". This is very true and has been proved right many a times. A person who is proud is so involved with himself that he fails to see life passing on without him and sooner or later falls flat on his face. On the other hand, a humble man without pride will find himself moving along with life.

A proud person has few friends, on the other hand a humble man will never find himself alone. Thus, pride must be avoided at all costs, no matter how high we have risen or how successfull we have become.

Life is a cycle and it does not take long for the person who is on top of the wheel to come swiftly down. On the other hand, the man who is down may soon find himself rising up the cycle of life. Thus we should never take undue pride in the fact that fate has allowed us to reach the top of the cycle but be humble knowing that soon enough the tide can turn and we could be taken back to the bottom. Similarly we should not feel disheartened if fate has conspired to send us to the bottom of the cycle for we can be sure that the wheel will turn and our hard days will be over and we will once again start rising up the ladder of life.

Covetousness

Covetousness is a blind desire for any object which we believe would make us happy. Every human has this aspect in his nature, some more than others. A covetous man can never be truly happy because he is for ever searching new items and belongings to covet. A person may covet material items such as a car, someone may covet a person, while another may covet a position in his office. We often exonerate covetousness thinking that desiring something is a natural aspect of human nature. But we should not make the mistake of substituting desire for covetousness. A healthy desire for something is natural. A teenager can very well desires a cycle or an I-Pod. Someone may desire a new mobile phone. Such natural desire are healthy and keep the person motivated to work hard to achieve this. But coveting something is totally different. It prevents the person from thinking straight and people go to all ends to possess the coveted item. That is why it is so dangerous and is classified as a sin.

Covetousness makes us blind to the consequences and we tend to succumb to our desires and become ready to do anything to attain the object of our desire. It can be overcome by practicing will power and being satisfied in the knowledge that we are doing whatever possible to get it. If the desire becomes over powering and we are unable to control this desire, it becomes covetousness which can prove to be destructive. The first step is to identify covetousness and differentiate it from normal human desire. Then we can practice our will power to isolate this unnatural desire and learn to live a happy contended life.

Lust

Lust here means any kind of passionate desire. We often mistake lust for sexuality, but it goes beyond that.

Commonly lust has two faces - lust for power and lust for the carnal pleasures. Both are detrimental to character formation and have to be controlled. From time immemorial man has a craving for power. In the early days, sons would kill their own fathers so that they could ascend the throne. This is the lust for power in its most brutal form.

Lust for sex is a commonplace even in today's world. Today sex has become so common that it is accepted in everyday life. Extra marital affairs, unwed parents, rapes, etc., are to be seen all around us. Man has descended to the level of animals in this particular sphere. This form of lust is the most dangerous. A lustful man is capable of any action to satisfy his lust.

This lust manifests itself in a desire to act without thinking of the consequences. It is often a violent trait arising out of frustration at the unfulfilled desires. Lust can be a retrograde factor if one is unable to rein in the pent up desires. Having said this, it must also be said that lust can also be a positive aspect of human nature if used constructively. Thus we should learn about our desires and curb those that we know are destructive. Obviously any sort of lust is undesirable if it becomes a part of our existence and becomes the main objective of our day to day life. We have to develop ways and means to control unbridled desires so that we can continue to live a life of contentment and happiness.

Greed

Greed is the most original of the above sins. Greed drives men and is the chief destroyer of human nature. Greed exists in all of us in varying degrees. It is how we tackle this innate human nature that defines us. Greed can exist in many forms be it materialistic or on a higher platform.

Greed is that quality which always makes us want more of everything. We usually think of a greedy man as a glutton. Yes gluttony is a form of greed, but there are more serious forms of greed. Chief amongst these are greed for money and greed for property. These are the three triumvirates of greed – food, money and property. All three when existing in uncontrollable quantities will ultimately destroy a person.

We are all familiar with the greedy man who eats more than he needs. He is unable to control his greed and overeats every time. The result is that he puts on more and more weight till he becomes obese and suffers from various diseases. It leads to an unhappy life, riddled with problems resulting in an untimely and probably painful death. The only way to control this greed is strict will power. Controlling ones diet and eating habits are discussed in full details later in this book.

Another equally serious form of greed is the greed for money. From childhood we grow up with the idea that money is the be all and end all of everything. We think that money can buy us everything. But we forget that happiness cannot be bought with money. Happiness comes from within and can never be bought or exchanged for money. If happiness could be bought, rich people all over the world would have been eternally happy. But the truth is that happiness is a state of mind. The poorest of poor may be happy while a man rolling in wealth may be an unhappy man. Of course this is not to say that money is not required or that an ambition to become rich is bad. But to make money the sole reason for existence is definitely not right. Money can buy us comfort, luxury, a sense of well being, even power, but it has its limitations. Thus a greedy man who runs after money at the cost of everything else is certainly doing himself a disfavour. We are aware that many of today's problems are because of man's eternal greed for money. Individuals, greedy for more money, succumb to illegal activities and end up becoming monsters propped up by all the cash they have earned. Companies looking to boost their profits are willing to do anything as long as it results in a healthy bottom-line. All this has a devastating effect on the personal life of the individuals involved and on society. Thus if we have money, we should enjoy it and make sure that we do not make it our master.

Greed for property is a big disease. For generations, individuals have been involved in bitter acrimony all for a piece of land. Families break up, brother kills brother and further people are willing to die rather than give up their piece of land. The number of frauds involving cheating the common man in land deals are well-known. Unscrupulous promoters become multi millionaires overnight by playing up to our greed for property. We should realise that land and property are only means to an end. A farmer needs land to till, people require a house to live in and industrialists need land to set up factories and so on. It is only when we think with a rational mind that we understand that having more land or property is not more important than alienating our kith and kin.

In fact it should be remembered that covetousness, greed and avarice all are more or less the same traits with slight variations.

Sloth

Originally sloth was described as the sin of sadness which included depression, uneasiness of the mind, etc. But in today's world sloth has been better described as the failure to utilise ones capabilities and talent. In common terms it is described as laziness. It is perhaps harsh on an individual who is naturally lazy to classify this as a deadly sin. But in early civilisation man was expected to work hard and contribute to society, and a failure to do so was looked down upon as a sin. Even in modern times, slothfulness prevents a man from finding his real place in society. A slothful man is looked down upon and rarely shines in his field. The doors of development and success are firmly shut for a slothful man. Each of us must, therefore, make an extra effort to be active in whatever we are doing, to constantly be on the move and avoid being slothful or lazy. We should use whatever talents we have, be it physical or mental to ensure that we always give the best of ourselves and be on the path of self improvement and success.

A lazy person just lumbers across the corridors of life, never finding what he wants and realises that all doors of opportunity are firmly shut in his face. Thus a person who feels that he is becoming slothful must shake off this feeling and get around to doing his work with full vigour and gusto. Then only can slothfulness be avoided and the peaks of success can be achieved.

Envy

Like all other original sins, envy is a deep rooted trait in man. Every person is envious of another who is better off than him. This envy often shows up in the way we behave and act. It can have a disastrous effect on the character of the man. An envious man is forever looking at others with a feeling of reproach and hatred. He becomes inward looking and ultimately destroys himself.

While envy is good in a way that it helps us to strive harder and to emulate the person who is having a better job, a better house, a better car and so on. But to burn within just because someone is living in pomp is retrograde. We should try to convert this negative feeling of envy into a positive one of emulating and work harder till we reach our goal. Then only we can conquer this sin and also take advantage of it.

Anger

"Anyone can become angry -- that is easy. But to be angry with the right person,

to the right degree, at the right time, for the right purpose, and in the right way -- that is not easy."

Aristotle 384 – 322 B.C..

Anger is described as an overwhelming feeling of annoyance or antagonism. Anger comes over us like a tidal wave and even we are not prepared for the consequences. All human beings have felt uncontrollable rage or anger at some time or the other. Even animals get angry from time to time. The difference between humans and animals are that humans have the power of logical thinking and can control their anger to a large extent.

A well-known dangerous sort of anger is the well-known 'road rage'. Road rage is the uncontrollable antagonistic feeling that comes over a driver when another who overtakes him, breaking the rules and then arrogantly speeding off. In such a scenario, even the calmest of men are known to be affected by road rage. They immediately speed up and stop at nothing to overtake the guy, even at the risk of having an accident and injuring or even killing themselves in the process. All logical thinking deserts them and their mind is possessed by one single thought - to get the better of the other guy.

Another dangerous form of anger is what is commonly known 'domestic violence'. Gruesome as it may sound this is an existing social evil even in today's modern world. A man is generally loving and considerate towards his wife and children. But when he perceives that he has been wronged, due to whatever reason, a violent anger comes upon him. His senses get blurred with emotion and he lets it out against the person thought to be the source of this - his wife.

The same feeling of being wronged, if directed against, say, a colleague, does not produce this sort of blinding anger, because in the first instance, the feeling of being wronged is increased multi-fold because it is against someone he loved and trusted, thus it is accompanied by a feeling of betrayal, which fans the fire of the anger. Secondly, it is a fact that although the anger has blinded his senses, he knows that his wife is defenseless and unlikely to retaliate, whereas a colleague would probably defend himself. Usually this brutal nature of the man generally surfaces when he is drunk, hence the social stigma is attached to alcohol consumption.

Anger is, simply put, a loss of control over one's emotions. Generally we put on a mask over our real feelings. But sometimes when the feeling is so intense, the mask is ripped open and the true nature is exposed. Thus anger can manifest itself in verbal abuse or physical violence.

All sorts of anger have negative effects on the body and the mind. It is a fact that anger causes headaches in many people especially suppressed anger. Thus it is necessary to release the anger in a non-violent manner. One of the ways to do this is to shout at the top of your voice. This lets out the feelings and calms you down considerably to the extent where your logic can take over.

Constructive Anger

Of course there is something known as constructive anger. Such an anger can be tapped by us to achieve our goals, to move forward and to get away from the clutches of laziness. Rightful anger is also useful in getting our point of view across to the individual who is encroaching on our rights. A mild man cannot voice his opinion forcefully and often finds himself relegated to the sidelines. An angry man on the other hand is able to deliver forcefully and ensure that his views are heard and acted upon. Even our children require doses of our anger from time to time so that they are aware of their limits. Mild parents are usually unable to control their children at all. This is not to say that we should get angry and beat up our children for no reason. But when the children know that the parents are angry with their actions, they will be less tempted to repeat them.

Anger is detrimental to health because it leads to hypertension and heart disease. Short tempered people who get angry easily are usually friendless and lonely. Thus it is important to learn to control and manage your anger.

ANGER MANAGEMENT

Managing ones anger is important in today's lifestyle when pressures are more, time is short and patience running thin. It is common to see the boss blowing steam. This is the reason anger management has become so important.

Managing our anger is all about understanding why we get so angry, what are the situations that make us angry and who are the people who tend to set off these angry feelings by their attitude, behaviour or talk. Once we have identified these situations and people with whom we get angry, it is a good idea to avoid them altogether or to develop strategies to prevent them from igniting your anger.

Ways to check your emotions

Some important ways to keep a check on your emotions when you feel increasingly angry are:

- Get away from the situation, if possible. Confrontation will lead to more anger and may end in violence. If you can get away from the situation keeping your dignity intact, then this is the best solution.
- Deep breathing is an excellent method to control your anger. Practice breathing deeply and slowly, counting slowly to ten or repeating a calming word or phrase, such as, "calm down," "take it easy," or "don't lose control".
- Close your eyes and imagine that you are in a place or situation that makes you feel peaceful, calm, and safe. Think about your loved ones, about the vacation you last had, etc. These thoughts will calm your mind and soon you will find your anger evaporating.
- Get some exercise. Try running, biking, walking, or dancing to calm your body so that you can think straight.
- Learn how to laugh at yourself and see humour in situations.
- Learn how to relax. Although you may have heard that expressing anger is better than keeping it in, frequent outbursts of anger are often counter-productive and may alienate others.
- Learn how to assert yourself. This is a constructive alternative to aggression. When you find yourself angry at another person, try to explain to them what is bothering you about their behaviour and why. It takes more words and work to be assertive than it does to let your anger show, but the rewards are worth it.
- Try to change the way you think. Angry people tend to curse, swear, or speak in highly colourful terms that reflect their inner thoughts. When you're angry, your thinking can get much exaggerated and overly dramatic. This is a negative thinking process. Try to replace this with a positive thinking process. When somebody yells at you, the best way to get angry is to think about the insult, the bad words, the rude gestures, and the unfairness of it all. Then you think about the person who is treating you this badly and slowly a deep aversion to the person and his words build within you, finally bursting in a fit of anger. Change the way you think when somebody blows his top. Think about the incongruity of it, the sorry picture he makes with all his angry words and body language. Tell yourself 'I will not follow this guy and make a fool of myself. I will preserve my dignity and keep my emotion in check'. You will find that it will be a lot easier for you to control yourself.
- Think logically. Analyse the situation and see whether you are being justified in getting angry at the person or situation which is causing this emotion. More often than not you will find that you are being illogical, that there is no logical reason that you are blowing

your top. True there may be reason for losing your cool, but not to the extent that you get into a rage and expose your emotions to all. When you think logically you will realise that it is better to get a grip on yourself and solve the problem rather than lashing out at others. Even if, as the case maybe sometimes, you come to the conclusion that you are right to get angry, the very act of logical thinking will cool your emotions and you will notice that your anger has reduced, allowing you to think better and control yourself and the situation.

If in spite of all the above, if you are still unable to control your anger, if it is having an impact on your relationships and on important parts of your life, it is time to consider counselling to learn how to handle anger better. A psychologist or other licensed mental health professional can work with you in developing a range of techniques for changing your thinking and your behaviour. They are trained to handle such situations and can assist you to lead a life with less anger, bitterness and rancour towards all around you. This is because anger is the most destructive of all human emotions, forcing people to act in ways that they will forever regret. Thus in spite of your best efforts if feelings of anger and hate overtake you it is advisable to go for professional help.

TIME MANAGEMENT

Time management is indeed as simple as it sounds – the management of the available time so that you make the most of it. Without proper time management techniques, an individual stumbles through life without aim or ambition, a piece of driftwood at the mercy of the wind and the waves.

The first step in effectively managing time is to develop an explicit statement of your long-range goals. Sit down in a quiet place with a relaxed frame of mind and think about your future and what you want to be and do in life. Now write down the points as they come to your mind. From this make a list of your long-term goals. This statement of goals will allow you to set shorter range goals and to prioritise specific activities depending on how much they contribute to your goals. Setting these long-range goals may be more difficult than you imagine. The process can force you to think about decisions that you have been putting off, or value issues that you don't want to handle and have been pushing to the background till now.

Write down your goals and tasks

Once you have your long-term as well as short-term goals written down, the rest will follow. Think about the effort required to achieve these goals. Now break it down to specific tasks that you set up for yourself. The following may be helpful in this respect:

"To do" List

Write down things you have to do, then decide what to do at the moment, what to schedule for later, what to get someone else to do, and what to put off for a later time period.

Daily/weekly planner

Write down appointments, classes, and meetings on a chronological log book or chart. Better still, chalk out your schedule first thing in the morning, check what's ahead for the day and always go to sleep knowing you're prepared for tomorrow. Make a routine for the day.

Long-term planner

Use a monthly chart so that you can plan ahead. Long-term planners will also serve as a reminder to constructively plan time for yourself.

Have realistic deadlines

The first thing any time manager would tell you is to have realistic deadlines for specific jobs as far as possible and then trying to keep it. There is no point in having deadlines that you cannot keep. There's no point in making commitments that are impossible to keep.

Take deadlines seriously

Remember, how you maintain your deadlines at office and at home influences how people view you. If you are the laid back type who never keeps a deadline, you are unlikely to have people taking you seriously. Once you give a deadline, you must attempt to keep it at all costs. That's why your initial appraisal of the deadline is so important. Treat deadlines the way you would like people to treat you, i.e., seriously. And when you fail to meet the deadline, explain why. Without giving lame excuses, accept responsibility and give the reason in a no-nonsense professional manner. You will find that people believe you depending on how you place the facts before them.

Be professional

You may wonder what being professional has to do with time management. In fact being professional has everything to do with time management and in fact every other sort of management.

If you have a professional attitude the first things that you ensure is to appreciate the value of time. Once you have committed a time frame, you should feel morally bound to stick to the time table. Being punctual, doing things on time is your way of telling the world that you are a true professional.

Programme your day and time yourself

It is worth your while to spend a few moments early in the day to think about your activities. Decide on your itinerary for the day. List out what you want to do, when you want to do and how much time you allocate to each activity.

Making a schedule is a good way of timing yourself. Write down the things to do, the time limits to do them in. Carry this little checklist with you and you will automatically find yourself getting more focused on the jobs that you have committed yourself to doing. Once you get used to following the time schedule, it becomes a habit and before long you will get into the habit of timing each activity and ensuring that you keep within the time frame allotted. Working to a time schedule is a great way of utilising the available time to the best advantage. Instead of stumbling through life without aim, you will find yourself making the maximum use of your time and getting the best out of the little time you have at your disposal.

Keep your table clean

This does not mean clearing the table and pushing the contents into the nearest available shelf or cupboard. It means attending to the work on your table and not allowing it to pile up. For if you do so, the work will be overbearing before long and you will be stifled and drowned with the overload. So, clear the papers as soon as they land on your table. Before you leave office for the day, go through the pending paperwork, clear what you can and leave the rest in an organised manner so that you can fruitfully attend to them first thing the next morning.

Most of us have been to offices where we have seen files piled up high on every table. An office which allows its employees to work in such a shoddy fashion, does not inspire confidence in their clients. The employees themselves adopt a lethargic attitude if they are allowed to procrastinate and postpone their jobs. Hence, the managers must ensure that everyone attends to every file as soon as possible and clear his work for the day before leaving the office.

Don't procrastinate

Procrastination is a curse. It is in fact a sort of diseasc which has pulled back a lot of people from attaining their goals. In simple words, procrastination means putting off for tomorrow what you can do today. This affects the best of us and the worst of us. Putting off for tomorrow what you should do today is the perfect way to forget about it altogether. Whether it is the payment of bills, answering mails or telephone calls, visiting friends and relatives or your routine office jobs, delaying the task should be totally avoided and is unacceptable.

Don't be a perfectionist

Nobody is perfect. Each individual comes with his or her own dead baggage which affects our performance. You have to understand your weaknesses and work on it. It is said that although perfection is desirable it is unattainable. In any given job, the idea is to do the best you can in the given time limit and move on. Striving for perfection in everything you do, will pull you back. The very job which you are trying to do so well, will be half done if you pour over the tiniest details. Thus it is better to accept that you are not perfect and leave it at that. Of course this does not mean that imperfect and incomplete work is acceptable, it just means that see the over all picture rather than jeopardising the whole work for a few tiny details.

Haste makes waste

Trying to do too many things in too less a time will invariably boomerang. Give yourself sufficient time to do each job. Don't push yourself too hard. By trying to do things too fast you will only end up making a mess of everything with disastrous consequences. Thus understand your own speed and work arround it. Some people are a lot more focussed, alert and competent than others. Everybody is not the same. Just because A can do a job in one hour, does not mean that you have to do it in 59 minutes. As long as you can finish the job and do it well you should be content.

Forget multi-tasking

Trying to do too many things at one time can lead to wastage of time. Have you not tried to read the newspaper while watching TV and talking on the phone at the same time? Result : all three tasks were done imperfectly. Neither did you remember what you read, nor what you saw on the TV, nor could you do justice to the pal of yours who called. Researches conducted in the University of Michigan proved that the percentage of errors doubled when participants tried to do two tasks at one time. According to the study, multi-tasking tires you out, gets even less done within the allotted time, is more stressful and leads to loss of focus.

Having said this, it is necessary to understand that many jobs require multi tasking. Thus multi tasking can sometimes be required in your job, studies etc. In such situations you cannot avoid this and the best you can do is to give your undivided concentration to the tasks.

Get off the Internet

The Internet is a mine of information if used to its full potential. At the same time it is easy to get sidetracked and waste valuable time in following irrelevant leads. Thus when you browse the Internet you should be clear about what you want to know, so that you do not waste time in aimless browsing. The unfortunate fact is that, the world over more time is wasted on the Internet than in any single activity.

The thumb rule when you are on the Net to find something specific is – do not digress from the topic. Many of us start on the Internet to look for some detail and end up spending the entire afternoon tracking something else altogether. In fact many offices track the Internet working time and browsing contents of their staff in order to reduce the time they waste on the Net. As useful as it is, it can be a deadly waste of time also. And by all means avoid chatting on the Net. The number of hours people waste in chatting to unknown people can be huge. Chatting is unproductive and an unnecessary waste of time. If you want to talk to your friends pick up the phone and talk to them. This way you can wind up in a few minutes instead of wasting hours.

Phone calls on the move

Reserve phone calls for when you are moving. For example, when you take your evening walk, it is a good time for social calls. In the office you need to stretch after being cooped up at your desk or hunched over the computer. Go for a short walk around. And use this time to make your calls. This way your time at your desk will not be wasted in idle chatter. And make it clear to your buddies that phone calls are welcome after office hours. When you are concentrating on serious work or at an important meeting or preparing a presentation it is a good idea to switch off the mobile phone in order to avoid distraction. But never make calls when driving. Your undivided attention should be on the road, do not allow yourself to be distracted by mobile calls when driving.

GIVE QUALITY TIME TO THE FAMILY

Man is a social animal and genetically tuned to living in social units. The strongest and most important of these units is the family. A man who has a happy family life is at peace with himself and the world. Thus it follows that any time management programme that you chalk out should include some quality time for the family. Maybe an hour or two in the evening spent in the company of your spouse and children, or on evening outing with them. Whatever it is, the time spent in the company of near and dear ones is time well spent. You will be better off mentally, emotionally and physically. If you are a busy executive who invariably comes home late, keep Sundays aside for the family. If your job requires you to travel for long periods leaving them alone, make up by going on vacations with them. Whatever it is, try to strengthen the bond with your family and you will be well rewarded throughout life.

And some for yourself

Every human being needs solitude. Some time which you can devote entirely to yourselves. A time when you look within yourself and reflect on life. Time doing such an activity is time well spent, for it is nutrition for the soul. Every person needs to contemplate on the track that his life is moving on. Do you have a goal in life? An aim, an ambition? Is it justified? Is it achievable? Are you driving yourself too hard? Do you need to tone down your ambitions? Are you giving enough time for yourself and your family?

Are you missing out on the simple joys of life? Think of the following - a beautiful flower, a child's sweet smile, a cat yawning, a moonlit night, the first rays of the rising sun, a melodious song, a thought provoking movie, an intellectually uplifting book, the chirping of birds, the tall trees swaying in the breeze, children playing in the street, the pitter patter of rain, fresh new leaves in spring and many other such sights. Do these have the power to uplift you, are they the source of quiet delight for you. If they do not bring joy to you then you may well be getting burnt out and need to take a break.

Now think when the last time you really noticed any of these beautiful sights. Can't remember? Never mind. In today's mad rush for materialistic pleasures most of us rush along in life looking for fame, wealth, fun and power. These are the goals of today's generation which is slowly and surely leading us to intellectual decay.

Next time you come upon any of the sights mentioned above, make an effort to pause. Stop whatever you are doing and enjoy the moment. Do it every time and soon you will be able to enjoy the subtle pleasures of life involuntarily.

In other words take time out for yourself. Step back from your hectic activities and ponder on life. No doubt money and fame are important, but that does not mean that you destroy yourself in its pursuit. Money is not the beginning and end of life. Consider it to be a means to an end. And the end is happiness. After all happiness is what you are after. If after leading a super hectic life and amassing a fortune, you end up with hypertension and diabetes due to your lifestyle, what have you gained? An old age riddled with health problems!

Thus it is so important to have the right perspective in life. You should try to lead a balanced life. Balance your life with the right amount of work and relaxation. You will find that you are better off for it. Make sure you have some time for yourself to spend the way you want to, to pursue your personal interests or hobbies and to further your intellectual self.

Family is important

Family is the personal preserve of every individual. From the time we were born, we are raised in a family atmosphere. This is the reason why man finds true happiness in the comfort and security of family life. Those who alienate themselves from their immediate family in pursuit of other pleasures and comforts will soon find themselves lost and lonely.

Humans by nature are social units and the smallest unit is the family. If the family breaks up we become individualistic and the very charm and beauty of life is lost on us. Thus it is important for us to lead a happy family life, so that we can co-exist with others in peace and happiness.

In today's mad scramble for money, power and prestige, the family often suffers. This is because the well being of the family comes last for the ambitious man who is more interested in making his career. Thus he has no time for his family. As time goes on and he achieves his ambition, he realises that he has failed to carry his family with him. He has alienated them and family values have broken down. Thus his dream becomes hollow for he has no one to share his joys and sorrows with. This is one of the major problems affecting our society today. Families are becoming nuclear, marriages are breaking up, old people find themselves leading a lonely life probably in an old age home and youngsters have no one to guide them through the crucial first stages of life.

Manage your job and family equally

Thus managing your job and family is one of the most important challenges of life. It is a seamless effort to balance both your job and family. Many big executives and businessmen do a wonderful job in their workplace. They achieve wonders and are acclaimed for their feats. Some are termed as 'bottom-line experts' – they manage to improve the profits of the company they work for, others are termed as 'turnaround experts' – they are experts in turning around loss making companies. Still others are termed as 'M & A Champions' – they are the guys who are good at acquiring companies. Whatever the term may be, these guys are good at their jobs and work wonders. They are very good at job management. However many of them are still unhappy.

The reason being that they are not able to manage their family life as well as their jobs. Due to this their families drift away from them, causing unhappiness. They find themselves in conflict with the members of their family. This can have two consequences - a life of agony for all members of the family or separation. In the first case, daily confrontation leads to depression. This has an effect on the job as they slowly become careless and less professional. Their work suffers and soon people forget that once they were the titans of the industry. They lose their self confidence and slowly fade away. In the second case they have to face the trauma of separation and the fact that their family life is a failure.

Thus it is obvious that you have to balance both your job and family. If the family life suffers, no one in that family can be truly happy. Similarly, if your job suffers, family cannot be happy because of the inherent tensions.

The question that arises is how do we go about balancing both our job and family life? The first mistake that people make is to consider job as being far more important than the family. Job is important no doubt, because without a job, the person faces financial difficulties, an insecure future and serious inferiority complex. Thus a steady job is one of the prime factors in the mental well being of the breadwinner. But the main point is that, job being one of the most important parameters in a person's life does not make the family inferior. Family holds a very important position in a human beings life and by neglecting the well being of the family, the entire existence of the person becomes meaningless. Family life should hold equal importance in the life of a person as his profeseion.

It is a proven fact that a person with a happy family life does not fall prey to the lifestyle diseases and does not become an alcoholic or a drug addict. The simple fact is that you have to maintain a balanced lifestyle if you are to keep your family happy. No man who returns home late night everyday can hope to have any sort of family life. Thus it is important to maintain a lifestyle that will give you enough time and energy to spend on the family.

The key is spend time with your family. Play with your children when they are young, guide and support them when they are older. Treat your spouse with respect, love and dignity. Be courteous and helpful to the elders in the family. Remember your children are watching you and learning from you. If you behave badly and irritably with your elders, one day your children will behave the same way with you and you will have only yourself to blame. But if you show love and respect to the elders by your own actions, they will also learn to treat you in the same manner.

Thus it is necessary to have a happy family life if you are to be truly happy in life. Family happiness is something which needs to be cultivated like a plant. It requires water and manure in the form of love, attention, sacrifice and devotion. A man who has cultivated family will never find himself alone.

BE HAPPY WITH YOUR JOB

The job you are doing assumes great significance since your world hinges around it. Someone who is not satisfied with his job can never hope to manage his life well. In today's world many people are unable to hold on to their jobs. For various reasons, they keep changing their jobs, some get better jobs, just drift from one job to the other job.

Let us begin by defining the word 'job'. The Oxford Dictionary defines job as 'a paid position of regular employment'. Thus job can be defined as a regular employment for which you are paid a monthly salary. People take up jobs as compared to business, because of the stability and assurance of a steady source of income. You are sure that as long as you do the job, you are going to be paid for it. Thus a job brings about a certain amount of stability in ones life.

In the olden times once a person got into a job, he spent the better part of his life in the same job. But today the scenario has changed completely. Today a person in the same job for years is seen as stagnating. Thus, every few years people change jobs out of compulsion, so that their career graph looks good.

The best way to enjoy the job you are doing is to do it diligently and sincerely. Whether you are a junior staff or an important executive, the idea is to do the best you can. Then you will be happy and confident. People respect someone who is good at his job. Even the junior most apprentice earns grudging respect from the top management of the company if he proves to be good at his job. There is no magic in this except hard work and diligence. Whatever be the job you do as long as you do it with full effort, you will satisfy yourself and your colleagues and co-workers. You must match your own expectations as well as the expectations of your seniors. This is what personal quality is all about.

CULTIVATE SPIRITUALITY

If I were asked to put an important quality that can define a man of character, it would undoubtedly be spirituality. Too often spirituality has been mistaken for religious fervour. Spirituality has nothing to do with religion and is all about finding oneself, it is about being what we are and not what others want us to be. A spiritual man essentially has most of the qualities stated above. A spiritual man is always guided by his inner mind. He finds solace in leading a simple life devoid of pomp and splendour. Spirituality does not mean that we have to cut off with our friends, stop socialising, start long drawn prayers or spend a lifetime in temples and other places of worship. Spirituality simply means understanding that life has a far bigger meaning than the material pleasures and desires and trying to find meaning in our day to day life.

A spiritual man is essentially a thinking man. How many times have we found ourselves sitting all alone and thinking of life, our future, the meaning of our existence and what we can do to make the world a better place to live in? There are very few people who have found time for this. Yet this is the essence of our life. Is what we are doing today necessary for us? Or are we so blinded by the glare of success and wealth that we are hurtling headlong into disaster? This is the question each one of us must ask and find our own answers. Life is very forgiving and gives us several chances to correct our path and tread in a path which will make us proud in the years to come.

Be happy

We all know that happiness is the goal of human life. This life is a precious gift to us from nature. Thus man instinctively seeks happiness, knowing that life is too short. Not only humans, all living beings spend their life in the pursuit of happiness.

You may well ask what an animal knows of happiness. Indeed, what do we know of happiness?

Our knowledge of happiness is usually restricted to the material senses. We are happy when we eat a good meal. We are happy when we possess wealth. We are happy when we achieve success and earn the respect of our peers. In the same way, an animal is happy when it has a good meal. A cat is happy when it is basking in the sun. A beetle is happy when it is lurking under a rock. Thus, different strokes for different folks!

It is a fact that all may not be happy with the same things. The feeling of happiness when we have a good meal may soon turn to guilt when we think of the consequences of having such a heavy meal. How many times have we heard the comment: "He may be rich, but he is not happy". But if wealth is a source of happiness, then how can a wealthy man not be happy? Of course, it all depends on the circumstances. A wealthy man who has worked too hard in earning the money is alienated from his family because he could not give them enough time. His wife after waiting for him all these years now decides to live it up and has a flamboyant lifestyle which does not please him at all. His children whom he did not guide properly because he was too involved in making money have gone astray. Can such a man ever be happy? No!! Such a man will one day regret that he has earned so much money but in the bargain has lost the love and affection of those who were nearest and dearest to him.

Similarly there are many examples which go on to prove that happiness is not a uniform item that can be guaranteed. The rishis of olden times described happiness as the absence of pain. A man who does not have any physical or mental pain is at peace with himself. But is he happy? A rock feels no pain, but can we call it a happy rock? The difference here is that a rock is an inanimate object whereas humans are capable of emotions of varying degrees. We all carry with us the baggage of our past actions. Thus when a man sits down to think, he is beset with doubts, fears, regrets and desires. All these are negative thoughts which cause pain thus it is said that the absence of pain itself is good enough to classify as being the source of happiness. Ancient wisdom is usually logical provided we devote the time and energy to think about it.

Happiness is something for which we are willing to go to any lengths. On achieving the object which was supposed to be the reason for happiness, we remain in that state for a short time only. Our mind then switches to something else which now becomes the object of our desires and which we believe may make us happy. Thus we go on a hunt again. This wild goose chase has been going on from time immemorial and will go on till eternity. In our wild pursuit of the elusive happiness we fail to realise that there are many small things on the way which could have made us happy. Our fixation for the object of our desire had made us blind to everything else.

Happiness is a state of mind

The fact is that happiness is a state of mind. We cannot define happiness. I have seen sadhus walking over burning coal. Their aim is to overcome the pain. They are forever trying to test their own limits. After meditating over life and its meaning they may have realised that human life is bound and restricted by pain of all kinds. They overcome emotional pain by total detachment from family and friends. They overcome physical pain by practicing rigorous yoga and punishing their bodies in various ways so that it learns to overcome the pain. They then try to enter the metaphysical state where they get ultimate happiness and joy.

This sort of strict discipline and punishment is not for ordinary people, but we can surely learn a lesson or two from this. The most important lesson is that it is not necessary to be happy at all times. Do not chase happiness, it is a frail master and the way is fraught with pain. Rather learn to get happiness out of small things. If you think deeply about your own life you will be amazed at how comfortable you are compared with those less fortunate than you. Your health, your family, your job, all of these should give you happiness. Even if your health, job or family life is not the very best, be happy with the million other things which give you joy. Life is beautiful and to be alive should be enough reason to make you happy.

WHO IS A HAPPY MAN?

A man who does not intentionally or unintentionally harm others is on the path to achieve happiness. There is something in us, some feeling which denies us happiness when we give sorrow or harm others. Of course there are many who revel in hurting others, whether physically, mentally or emotionally. But they are exceptions as well. Many may not empathise with another's sorrow, but being the source of the sorrow is something else altogether.

Whether as a child, a teenager, an adult, a businessman, a professional or a labourer, a hard working man who has been sincere in his job is always satisfied at the end of the day. When we know that we have earned the bread we are eating by the sweat of our brow, the bread is bound to taste sweeter. A cheat or a shirker is always troubled by pangs of guilt over his nature which restricts him from being happy.

Although it is passé, it is a fact that truthfulness helps to achieve happiness. When we lie and cheat, our body is not at rest. Our pulse, heartbeat, etc., is raised and the body releases certain hormones. This is what the narco-analysis is all about. It detects these unnatural signals from the body and comes to know whether the person is lying or saying the truth. Our mind and body are sanguine when we speak the truth, but undergo certain changes when we lie. These very changes affect our behaviour, making it difficult for us to be happy under the circumstances.

BE COMPASSIONATE

Compassion is one of the most noble traits in a man's character. A compassionate man is one who sincerely cares for the well being of others and suffers when he sees others suffering.

I have earlier spoken about empathy and sympathy. Compassion is the end product. People around us all have their own problems. For a person to put aside his problems and spend time in trying to solve another's problems is the sign of a compassionate man. Compassion can be of many types, but to be sincere, compassionate words must be followed up by suitable action. Most of us do not have the time, the inclination or the resources to attend to another's problems. So we develop a cynical attitude where we make ourselves believe that every person is responsible for his own troubles and must solve it himself. Such a person has turned away from compassion and has become selfish, self centred, cynical and bitter in his attitude towards others.

Today it is old fashioned to talk of compassion and empathy, etc. Unfortunately, society today has become so materialistic that each of us live in our own ivory tower. Far from being compassionate many people today use and abuse others in their quest for a more luxurious life, a better job, promotions and other materialistic cravings. It is not a sin to seek a better life for oneself, but while doing so if we can show some compassion for others who we leave behind on the way, life would take on a different meaning for us.

On the other hand, there are many for whom compassion is only a lip service. Many of our politicians, leaders, etc., exhibit this trait. They show a false sense of empathy and compassion. But they cannot fool people for ever. A leader who has true compassionate feelings towards the common man, will find them reciprocating and his popularity will rise. On the other hand people who pretend to show compassion are soon caught and their insincerity is also soon evident and their popularity reduces.

We have learnt from Mother Teresa the value of true compassion. Of all the characteristics that make a true human being, the most important is compassion. Compassion for another human being, compassion for those not as fortunate as we are, compassion for the weak and oppressed, these are noble traits indeed. True happiness lies in being compassionate, in giving others who are in need. Of course all of us cannot be like Mother Teresa, but if we do whatever we can in our own way, this will also bring us peace and solace which are the pillars of happiness.

Listen to your inner voice

Humans have this great intuition of an inner voice which guides them and helps them determine what is right and wrong. It is important for each of us to listen to this small voice within us. It may be a pang of guilt, it may be a second thought, but without doubt whenever we embark on a wrong path, this voice guides us. Those who listen to this voice will certainly be on the way to happiness, those who ignore will do so at their own peril. Thus it is important for us to cultivate this and help our inner self to guide us at all times.

Finally, life is beautiful. We are fortunate that we are among the few who have the ability and resources to enjoy the beauty of life. Let us not spoil it for ourselves, for others and for future generations.

"Truth is victorious, Never untruth.
Truth is the way;
Truth is the goal of life,
Reached by the sages who are free
From self-will"

—Mandaka Upanishad 3.1.6

***

9

CRISIS MANAGEMENT

"A leader or a man of action in a crisis almost always acts subconsciously and then thinks of the reasons for his action."
– Jawaharlal Nehru

The word "crisis" is defined by the dictionary as 'a time of danger or great difficulty'. The concept of crisis management is to have the requisite knowledge, skill and aptitude to tide over this difficult time.

In our day to day life we are faced with many crisis situations. The most common ones are described here with useful ideas on how to prepare for, cope with and overcome the crisis.

BEWARE OF FIRE

"Fire is a good servant but a bad master". This truism has been proven and it can have disastrous consequences if it goes out of control. There can be fire in the kitchen due to faulty appliances, in the house due to carelessness or even due to faulty equipment.

The most common area of fire is the kitchen. Every kitchen has the potential for breeding a fire. People working in the kitchen should be aware of and take adequate precautions to ensure that there are no accidents due to unsafe of fire. The following points will be of help:

1. Synthetic clothing is a no-no in the kitchen. Synthetic clothes and curtains are fire hazards and must be kept far from the kitchen. People working in the kitchen should wear cotton clothes. Synthetic curtains must be removed.
2. The kitchen must not be left unattended with the gas flame on. There are cases where the kitchen has been left unattended and the ensuing fire was not detected till too late.
3. Ensure that a fire extinguisher is placed just outside the kitchen. This will help in putting out small fires before they become large and unmanageable. It is not enough just to place a fire extinguisher. The operation of the extinguisher must be known to all. Further the extinguisher must be serviced on an annual basis so that it is ready for use at all times.
4. The best treatment for a burn is normal running water. Water helps in removing the heat from the burnt area and will ensure that blistering is to a minimum.

5. Every kitchen must be stocked with a burn ointment which must be applied immediately after putting the burnt area under running water. The ointment will ensure protection from bacteria and prevent infection of the affected area.

6. For serious burns it is better to avoid water due to the chances of a secondary infection due to the bacteria which may be present in the water. In this case the best action is to remove the pieces of clothing stuck to the burnt area, if possible and cover with a burn dressing. If a burn dressing is not available, the best option is to liberally apply the burn ointment and then cover with sterile gauze. The patient should be taken to a hospital for treatment immediately.

7. The nearest treatment centre for burns must be known and contact details must be available readily so that in case of a burn immediate help is available.

CUTS AND WOUNDS

Many of us will be exposed to cuts and bruises whether at home or in the workplace and it is necessary to know the immediate first aid actions. In case of a cut where extensive bleeding has taken place, the first action is to elevate the bleeding part and apply a tourniquet. A tourniquet should be applied at the nearest artery so that arterial bleeding can be reduced immediately.

For a severe cut on the hand a tourniquet should be tied just above the elbow. For a cut on the leg a tourniquet must be tied around the upper thigh. These are areas where the major arteries lie close to the surface and by putting pressure on the artery, bleeding can be reduced. Any long piece of clothing or a rope or belt can be used as a tourniquet in an emergency. It should be tight enough to put direct pressure on the artery and thereby control the bleeding.

But it must be remembered that a tourniquet must be loosened after a few minutes so that normal blood flow can resume to the affected limb, otherwise the tissues will die due to lack of blood and oxygen.

Any severe cut must be taken with utmost seriousness and the patient should be rushed to the nearest hospital or dispensary, after first aid has been given. Even if the bleeding appears to have stopped the patient must be taken to the care centre for any necessary stitching, dressing and medication.

LOSS OF A LOVED ONE

This is one of the most traumatic crisis situation that can affect any household. The pain and emotion that the members of the family experience during this difficult period cannot be explained in mere words. People are usually at a loss for words and feel uncomfortable in such situations. But we cannot run away from the scene and have to bravely confront the crisis.

As a responsible member of the family, we must set aside our deep sorrow and pain and ensure that the others are consoled and looked after. We can reconcile ourselves with our pain later on but the need of the moment is to identify the person who is most likely to crack and offer him or her the maximum support so that the person does not break down permanently. Food and water must be provided so that the grieving family members are not starved. Sleep deprivation is one of the major causes for illness during such cases and everybody must be reminded to sleep on time.

People who are on medication often forget their medication and must be reminded to take the same on time in order to prevent complication thus leading to another crisis.

Individual counselling may be necessary for the most affected person. Mothers and wives are the ones who are most affected and special care must be given to them. The method and type of counselling and condolence cannot be explained here, as it depends on the individual concerned, but very often, just being nearby and saying a few soothing words help. Do not be over bearing or over sympathetic, sometimes silence can also send vibes of comfort. A hug, a clasp of the shoulder, a pat on the head, a kiss on the forehead can all be gestures of comfort and companionship, likely to lend solace to the grieving person.

Many well wishers have the habit of asking the person about details of the demise of a loved one. Avoid this as the person lives through the trauma every time he or she answers such a question. Instead find something good to say about the person who is no more. This will give some solace to all concerned. And never say, 'he has lived long enough, it was time to go'. Even if a person lived till a hundred years old, it may not seem long enough for his loving children, so avoid such sweeping statements.

FINANCIAL CRISIS

A financial crisis is one of the most undesirable disasters that can strike any family or individual. While other difficulties can usually be overcome, a financial crisis is like a cancer spreading its tentacles to all facets of life, finally destroying the family. This is the reason that any financial crisis must be tackled with utmost urgency.

Statistics for the last several years have shown that the number one reason for suicides across the world over is finance. In other words, when the family has no money for their day to day survival, sometimes the ultimate option may seem the best.

But it is a known fact that difficult times will come and go. No one should throw in the towel and escape. Any financial crisis must be faced with courage and equanimity. A qualified person who suddenly finds himself jobless and unable to fend for himself and his family should not baulk at taking up any job available, even menial jobs to tide over the crisis. Ultimately life has to go on and our endeavour should be to keep on trying for a better life.

The current financial crisis has hit the entire globe in a big way. People who bought fancy houses, running up huge debts in the bargain, found the current value of the houses less that half of the price they bought for. On top of that, job lay offs and salary cuts became common place putting a heavy strain on finances. People who used to live a life of luxury depending on the famed credit cards suddenly found their lifelines cut as banks stopped or reduced their credit worthiness.

Avoiding financial crisis

In everybody's life there could be times when one faces a financial crisis. Although such situation have to be faced with equanimity it is always better to prevent such situations with some planning and financial discipline. The following points will help in this respect.

AVOID LIVING ON CREDIT

Even if you possess a credit card use it only for emergency purchases and for those times when you urgently want to purchase something, and find that you do not have money in your wallet.

Use that credit card only when really needed

Avoid making big- ticket purchases on your credit card. Big purchases e.g., refrigerators, TV, etc., must be planned in advance and only if you have the resources to pay for the same. There is no point in mortgageing your future in order to upgrade your present lifestyle.

Make timely payment of your credit card balances

Make sure you clear your entire credit card balance every month. The first sign of a financial crisis stalking you is the carry forward of the balance amount on your credit card. Remember interest rates go up as you carry forward the balance. Further this is the sign of an avalanche of debt coming your way. If you are unable to pay the full outstanding balance on your card at any point of time, you must stop any further use of the card till such time that you are able to fully pay the balance. This way you will be controlling your debt and avoiding a spiralling effect which will ultimately become uncontrollable.

CHECK YOUR PAYING CAPACITY BEFORE GOING FOR A HOME LOAN

One of common type of loans is a housing loan, because it is easily available and well marketed. Although a home loan is a wonderful opportunity for everyone to own their own home, please be sure to calculate your EMI and ensure that you will have the capacity to repay the loan month on month for the next twenty years or more. If there is even an iota of doubt, postpone the purchase of the house or go for a smaller loan. And remember if the interest rates go up, your EMI will increase, or your payback period may increase. These variables have to be factored in when you go for a big loan.

Do you really need that car?

Another tempting purchase where a loan is easily available and which people go for without calculating their paying capacity is a car loan. Once again be sure to calculate the EMI and your repayment schedule before you jump in. If you feel there would be any problem in this, it is better to stick to the two wheeler or the small car and be debt free.

EMIs MAY MEAN MONTHLY TROUBLES

As a thumb rule remember that the total of all your EMIs and credit card balances should be less than your savings after their payments. In other words, your total EMI must be less than half of your total disposable income after allowing for every expense in the house including a kitty for emergency situations. This way you will have enough and more for loan repayment and have something left over for your monthly savings.

SAVE FOR THE RAINY DAY

Be like the proverbial ant, saving for the rainy day at every opportunity. Although at this point of time everything appears to be normal, one never knows when disaster can strike and crisis management is all about being prepared for the worst case scenario.

If, in spite of your best efforts, you do find yourself in a financial crisis, there is no need to panic. Make sure to maintain your calm, discuss with you near and dear ones on the best course of action. If some loans are to be repaid, it is better to borrow from a family member, if possible and then repay the amount thereby reducing your liabilities. Cut down on your lifestyle maintainance expences, if necessary sell off your house and car, but do not think this to be the end of the world. As long as you have your life there will always be opportunities to bounce back. Tide over the crisis, do not cave in and soon you will find that the winds of fortune will start blowing your way again, your sails will billow and you will start moving once again towards better shores.

MEDICAL CRISIS AND FIRST AID

A sudden medical emergency is something which everybody dreads but it can strike anytime. Every person must make sure that he has medical insurance for himself and the family members since a medical crisis can strike without warning. Having a health insurance ensures that you are ready and prepared for any expense that the medical treatment may entail.

It pays to know a bit of first aid and immediate actions required till the patient is in the hospital or under the treatment of a doctor. Given below are some of the common ailments that can strike us at any time and the immediate actions to be taken prior to medical treatment.

ARTIFICIAL RESPIRATION AND CPR

It is necessary for everyone to know the basics of artificial respiration and Cardio Pulmonary Resuscitation (CPR). Knowledge of these basic procedures well enable you to save someone's life one day.

A person may become unconscious and his breathing may stop due to any one of the following reasons. The list is not exhaustive and there may be more unknown reasons that can cause a cessation of breathing.

1. Major allergic reaction
2. Poisons inhaled or swallowed
3. Drug overdose, alcohol or sleeping tablets
4. Suffocation due to gas or smoke
5. Blast injury causing damage to lungs
6. Coronary Thrombosis (also known as myocardial Infarction or Heart Attack)
7. Other unknown reasons causing a person to become unconscious with breathing stopped

The first and immediate action is to observe if the casualty has any external injuries or bleeding from the mouth or nose. In such a case it is advised to keep the casualty as comfortable as possible till medical help arrives.

If there are no signs of any external injury then an immediate attempt should be made to restore breathing. The procedure is as follows :

1. The first action is to clear the airway of any obstruction. This is immediately done with the casualty lying flat on his back, tilting the head backwards while lifting the chin upwards. This will move the tongue forward and clear the airway.

2. Any debris in the mouth should be cleared and mopped out by means of a handkerchief or a piece of clean cloth. Dentures, if any should also be removed.

3. If the casualty is still not breathing artificial respiration should be commenced at once. The procedure is as follows:

   - pinch the casualty's nose with the thumb and index finger.

   - seal your lips around the patients mouth and blow into his mouth till you see the chest rising (you may use a handkerchief between your lips and his mouth).

   - Give two such quick inflations and see whether there is any improvement in the casualty.

   - If there is some improvement in the colour of the face and lips or if there is a feeble breathing, continue with the inflations at the rate of about twelve inflations per minute.

4. If there is still no improvement, check for the pulse. The carotid artery at the neck is the best for checking the pulse. You may also place your ear at his heart and check for any sounds of heart movement.

5. If no pulse or heart beat is heard, CPR must be commenced immediately preferably by a trained first aider. CPR is done as follows :

   - place the casualty on a hard surface lying with face up and head tilted backwards.

   - cardiac massage is given by placing the hands on the middle of the lower half of the breast bone and pressing for half second duration – hundred times a minute.

   - after fifteen compressions, artificial respiration is given for two inflations.

   - If two trained people are available, then one person can give the cardiac massage for five times and then the second person gives the artificial respiration for five times.

   - If the heart starts to beat, the colour of the face and lips will improve and the pupils will get smaller. Also a feeble pulse and heart beat can be heard. In such a case the CPR is continued till the heart beat improves. Then the heart compression is stopped but the artificial respiration is continued till the casualty is breathing normally.

6. Although a CPR is to be preferably given by a trained first aider, it may happen that you are the one and only person on the spot

with no help in sight. In such a case it is better to start the CPR at the earliest possible time instead of helplessly watching the deteriorating condition of the casualty.

7. In all cases the casualty is to be transferred to a hospital or under a doctor's care as soon as possible.

***

10
ENVIRONMENT MANAGEMENT

> *"There is a sufficiency in the world for man's need but not for man's greed."*
>
> *Mohandas K. Gandhi*

The degradation of the environment is a matter of prime concern to all. If the environment is not protected, the world will suffer from a number of disastrous effects and will finally result in the extinction of life on earth. We have to remember that the environment is ours and we must save the earth. If we destroy our planet we will have nowhere to go. Thus saving the environment is in our interest and we should do the utmost to protect the earth from pollution and damage.

Environment management is what we need at this crucial hour. Each one of us can make a difference to the environment. By following a few simple rules and disciplining ourselves, we can make earth a n environmental friendly place.

The first and most important cardinal principle of environment management is : Do not waste. Whatever we use or require are part of the earth's resources. Wastage of any sort is wastage of the scarce resources, whether it be water, food, fuel, clothes, or anything else. Man has a tendency to waste and the tons of garbage that we see piled up is proof enough of this. If man uses all the resources he has without any wastage the world would have been a much more environment friendly than what it is today.

WATER

Take the case of water. All of us are guilty of wasting water. Water is definitely a scarce resource, Whether it be ground water, river water or rain water. By using only the amount that is needed, we can surely ensure a better world for our future generations.

Wastage of Groundwater is worrisome. Groundwater is a scarce commodity and is renewable only during the monsoons. Falling groundwater level is causing a decrease in ground pressure and is leading to subsidence. Further in coastal areas, falling groundwater level is compensated by seepage of sea water, making the whole water table brackish and unfit for human consumption. Thus we must, at all costs preserve and conserve groundwater. In today's cities rainwater does not find enough open spaces to seep into the ground so even this is limited. Big cities have huge apartment blocks which have a never ending thirst for water. Most of these blocks have the facility for pumping up both groundwater and pipe water supplied by the water corporation.

The most obvious way to do this is to limit the use of groundwater. Groundwater should be used only for drinking and cooking purposes and as a backup, should the piped water supply fail. There should be a system of refilling groundwater during the monsoons. Depending on nature to do this is simply not enough especially in cities. Rain catchment areas should be set up where rainwater can quickly find its way to the water table. Rain water harvesting is a good way of ensuring that the water table gets filled during the monsoons and as such in the drier areas rain water harvesting must be made mandatory.

PIPED WATER IS ALSO A SCARCE RESOURCE

Many of us think that piped water can be used carelessly. Well, that is a wrong perception. Afterall the river from where it is taken is in any case going to dump the entire water into the sea. Thus we think that a bit of wastage will do no harm. We forget that it costs the government a lot of effort to purify the water and pump it to our homes. River water is impure and cannot be pumped directly for our consumption. The cost of purification in terms of cost of equipment, power, labour, etc., should be kept in mind. Again there is a huge cost of transporting the water to our homes, the cost of pumping it up to the reservoir, etc. When I say cost, it does not mean that those who can afford it can waste. By no means. Water, power, etc., are all heavily subsidised by the government. Even where it is not subsidised, paying for it will not cover the cost of nonrenewable energy used for purifying the water and pumping it to our taps.

And we should not forget that any sort of nonrenewable energy results in global warming and wastage of the scarce resources. Thus reduction of energy spending will directly reduce global warming.

In many countries desalination plants are the source of potable water. The effect of wastage is maximum in these countries which spend an enormous amount of time, labour and cost for desalinating, purifying and transporting this to the taps in areas where there is neither Groundwater nor any river flowing nearby.

We should, therefore, make an effort not to waste water and conserve this scarce resource. Whether during brushing our teeth, washing utensils and clothes, bathing, cooking, etc., a bit of effort to close the tap when not required, will go a long way in making the world a better place.

ENERGY

Inefficient utilisation of fossil fuel is perhaps the biggest culprit in destroying the environment.

It is a nonrenewable source of energy, which means that wastage of fossil fuels will result in an ultimate shortage of the same thus threatening our future generations to untold misery and suffering if the existing pool of fossil fuels run out. In such a situation, we should try to come up with a suitable and affordable sources of energy. There is no doubt that as the stock dries up, the price of fuel will go through the roof resulting in spiralling inflation and this will wipe out the wealth of the common man as well as nations. Unscrupulous dealers will always play with the price of essential commodities such as fuel —the moment they see the demand picking up and supply not meeting, they will start stocking up on the particular commodity and start speculative trading which will drive the prices sky high.

This is exactly what happened in the months of June to October 2008 when the price of crude oil went soaring up to hit a high of US$ 150 per barrel. This was not the natural price. Within the next one month the price of crude oil plummeted between US$ 45 and US$ 60. Of course, the global recession and the subsequent belt tightening by the industry as well as the end users drove the demand down which assisted the free fall. But the price will not move up once again albeit at a more mature price. As demand picks up, supply reduces due to drying up of existing oil wells, we will once again see a spike in prices. Thus we should take the hint and cut down on unnecessary wastage of this precious commodity.

Fossil fuels have other major disadvantages. They release noxious fumes. This is not only harmful for health it also leads to global warming. Today our biggest challenges are the depletion of the ozone layer and global warming. Depletion of the ozone layer will increase the amount of harmful ultraviolet radiation and will have far reaching and disastrous consequences on life on earth. Global warming as we all know will lead to climate changes, melting of glaciers, increase in the sea water level and will ultimately wipe out life from our planet. Thus these are very serious issues and can only be resolved if each one of us do our bit to conserve the fossil fuels as well as switch to renewable sources of energy where feasible.

PRESERVING NONRENEWABLE SOURCES OF ENERGY

There are many ways of preserving nonrenewable sources of energy and efforts have been made many times over. Usage of public transport, pool cars, company buses, even walking where the distance is short, will all help in the conservation of the fossil fuel. Better driving habits, making sure that the vehicle is well maintained, even keeping track of the tyre pressures will reduce the consumption.

Switching to renewable sources of energy will definitely be a boon for the environment. We are blessed with an abundance of solar energy, wind energy and tidal energy. We should learn to harness these in the most suitable way. Leadership for this must come from the industry who should realise that it is time that they stopped making society pay for increasing their bottomline. They should make a concerted effort to save the environment and not disfigure our beautiful planet for monetary gains.

NUCLEAR POWER - THE GOOD NEWS

The good news is that we are now on the verge of an exciting alternate source of energy - nuclear power. With India having signed the nuclear treaty with the United States of America, the way is clear for us to proceed aggressively with developing nuclear power for civilian use. India has ambitious plans in this field and one hopes that within the next ten years the share of nuclear power in our total power generation capacity will go up substantially. Nuclear power is a clean fuel. The only drawbacks are the safety of the reactors and the disposal of nuclear waste. The world is forging ahead with this new technology to meet both these concerns and it is hoped that suitable solutions to these will be found soon.

Along with nuclear energy, thegovernment should also promote the use of renewable sources of energy so that our dependence on fossil fuels is considerably reduced with the passage of time.

WASTE MANAGEMENT

The management of waste is a crucial part of any environment management system and is not to be taken lightly. Whether it is from the factories, from offices or from homes, humans generate an alarmingly high amount of waste. Managing this waste and its proper disposal has proved to be a difficult task for city planners. Many cities use the waste for landfill purposes. While this is a good way to dispose of the waste, it is not the most economical. Household waste contains a large amount of organic matter which can be treated to provide energy on the one hand and fertilizer on the other hand. Unfortunately our present day city municipalities have not devoted much time and energy to this aspect and thus the waste is either dumped into garbage vats to rot, burnt off or used as landfill. With city population rising along with a proportionate increase in the amount of garbage generated, it is time to invest in a technology which will convert this waste into usable energy while at the same time produce the much needed fertilizers for our farmers.

The best method of handling waste management is the three R's:

- Reduce

- Reuse
- Recycle

It is only if the above solutions are followed can there be any fruitful efforts at waste management.

Industries should also spend more on managing their waste instead of dumping their noxious chemicals and untreated waste into the nearest river. Even our modern day hospitals lack any sort of viable waste management policy resulting in hospital waste lying around, contaminating the environment, getting into the water table etc.

If we do not take immediate action to manage our waste in a more concerted manner, we will soon find ourselves neck deep in garbage, filth and industrial waste. Thus it is time for us to stop treating our beautiful planet as our backyard where we callously dump our waste. This is especially true for big cities. They generate waste at an alarming rate which is often more than the removal capacity of municipality. The solution is not the disposal of the waste. What is required is a practical blue print for waste management.

Waste recycling is an important aspect of any waste management plan. At least 50 % of non-organic waste can be recycled. Almost 100 % of organic waste can be converted to bio gas and fertilizers. This is no rocket science, what is needed is some will power from the authorities coupled with some pragmatic implementation.

Any good waste management plan must start from the bottom of the pyramid - the generation of waste. City dwellers must be educated and made aware of the hazards of waste, so that they generate less waste in the first place. The positive aspect is that more waste is generated from well to do houses than from the houses of those who are economically weaker. This means that the section of people who need education in waste management are those that have the ability to understand and appreciate this.

A final thought on waste management - let us all pledge today to reduce the outflow of waste from those places we control - our homes, our offices and places of business. Let us pledge not to leave our rubbish behind wherever we go, whether in parks, public places or on holidays. Remember the thrust for effective waste management must come from the people. Then only can the authorities do their bit and make our cities and our planet a cleaner place for all of us to dwell in.

GREENING THE EARTH

For the last two or three centuries, the western world has been developing and industrialising at a rapid pace. The brunt of this had to be borne by our mother earth as forests are flattened, agricultural land taken over and all vestiges of greenery practically removed from cities. It is only now that when industrialisation has hit a plateau that the developed countries have taken an interest in the green cover of the earth. Countries like India and China are still in the developmental stage and should resist the tendency to relegate the environment to the backyard, just as the western world did a few decades back.

It is the greenery of the earth that regulates the Carbon Dioxide - Oxygen balance. They also regulate the rain cycles and act as natural dust catchers. In addition, trees play a big role in the balance of temperature on our plant. They reduce the effects of global warming and act against soil erosion, top soil depletion, etc.

Everybody knows and appreciates the value of the green cover. But even then green is a dirty word in the industry and green environmentalists are looked down upon as scourges who are against development. But we should understand that the green cover of the earth plays a very important part in the life cycle. By destroying the natural forests and trees we are laying an irreversible path for our own destruction. Needless to say development is an essential part of any country's progress and should not be halted at any cost. At the same time the players in this game must realise the importance that greenery plays and respect the green cover. If trees have to be felled in the name of development, so be it. But the trees felled must be compensated by planting an equal, if not more number of trees at other suitable locations.

If we as individuals and the industry as a whole respect the values of trees and forests, the battle is half won. It is time that we play a greater role against the felling of trees and take a balanced and pragmatic approach towards development. Without stopping development at any cost we should find ways and means to keep the green cover of the earth intact. Too much has been lost and it is now time to halt. Developing countries will no doubt cry foul but we have to face the realities at some time or the other. Developed countries should have a system for compensating the developing countries for slowing down their industrialisation for the sake of greenery.

This would be the opportunistic moment for all of us to take a pledge. A pledge to plant trees whenever and wherever possible, and a pledge to protect the environment. Only by living up to what we have pledged can we ensure that we hand over this wonderful planet of ours to the next generations in good condition as we inherited it.

***

11

PERSONAL GROOMING

> *"The mirror is a worthless invention. The only way to truly see yourself is in the reflection of someone else's eyes."*
>
> *–Voltaire*

Personal grooming is an inherent part of lifestyle grooming. Lifestyle grooming is all about having a lifestyle which will ensure that you are healthy, happy and wealthy. Personal grooming, on the other hand, has to do with your personal hygiene, dress sense, etiquette and so on. We live in a society in which most people are obsessed with beauty, celebrities, style and brand names. Thus, to make a mark, one has to pay close attention to personal grooming in order to ensure that one is not left behind in the race to success.

PERSONAL HYGIENE

Personal hygiene is something which all of us must pay special attention to. This affects every moment of our life, it affects our relationships with others and also affects the way others see us. Personal hygiene by its very name suggests that we should keep ourselves clean at all times. This is very true in a country like India, where heat and dust are an essential part of outdoor life.

The following points are to be noted in order to maintain personal hygiene

Oral hygiene

Teeth should be brushed ideally after every meal. This is impractical and may be even detrimental to the enamel if done too many times. Take care to brush your teeth at least twice a day. Brushing before going to bed is important in order to avoid accumulation of bacteria in the mouth during the night. These bacteria emit a foul smell which remains even after morning brushing. Thus people who do not brush their teeth even properly or brush only once a day may suffer from bad breath.

Brushing your teeth twice a day and cleaning your tongue is good enough to relieve you of bad breath. If it still persists, there are a few home remedies.

Fenugreek tea: This remedy has been known to cure bad breath. Fenugreek tea (although, it is not tea, strictly speaking) is made by boiling one teaspoon of Fenugreek (methi) seeds in half a litre of water for fifteen minutes, straining it and drinking the same as tea. Fenugreek tea has other benefits including regulating blood sugar and blood cholesterol levels, treating constipation, gout, indigestion, muscle pain and poor appetite. Unfortunately, fenugreek tea also has a few side affects especially for people suffering from allergic reactions and those who are on medication. Thus, it is advisable to consult your physician before starting off on this miracle tea.

Mouthwash of parsley and clove : Parsley is another natural cure for bad breath. Boil a few sprigs of chopped parsley and a few cloves in two cups of water. Gargling with this mixture after every meal has been known to rid bad breath.

There are other measures such as, eating guava, consuming juice of raw fruits or vegetables, drinking enough water, avoiding smoking, which may cure bad breath. But there is no doubt that good oral hygiene is the best remedy. Thus, brushing your teeth and cleaning the tongue are best remedies. If bad breath still continues in spite of this, then there is some other serious problem and it is time to visit your doctor.

Body odour

When two people are in close proximity, it is body odour which hits them first. Even before they introduce themselves, their body odour travels ahead. Some people suffer from severe body odour and need to do something to reduce it. Unlike what is shown in TV commercials, spraying a deodorant may not always be the best way to fight body odour.

Body odour is mainly caused by bacteria on the skin as a result of sweating. The most susceptible areas are the armpits and the genitals as these areas are usually covered and in addition, they produce proteins and oily substances on which bacteria thrive. The feet also produce bad odour because they are wrapped in shoes and socks, thus allowing fungi and bacteria to flourish. Thus, poor hygiene is the most common cause for body odour.

Body odour may also be due to a variety of other reasons. People who take strong medicines may have a specific body odour. Diabetic patients may smell of Acetone because of the insulin they take. People who smoke or drink excessively may have an unpleasant body odour. Body odour may also be due to some serious illnesses such as, kidney or liver disease, fungal infections, etc.

Reducing body odour: The best remedy for body odour is to observe good hygiene and cleanliness. Applying anti-perspirant or odious quantities of powder should be avoided as they clog up the sweat glands. Using an anti-bacterial or a deodorant soap can combat body odour due to sweating. Having a shower after returning home on a hot day is no doubt one of the best remedies as it washes off the sweat, the bacteria and the body odour.

Dietary habits: There is no doubt that diet affects body odour. What you eat will define how you smell to a certain degree. Red meat releases toxins into the blood stream causing body odour, hence regular consumption should be avoided. Avoiding excess consumption of alcohol, caffeine, garlic, etc., have been found to be helpful in reducing body odour. A healthy and balanced diet of whole grains, leafy vegetables, fresh fruits, sprouts, etc., will not only reduce body odour but help you to keep fit at all times.

Clothes: One of the causes of body odour is repeatedly wearing the same unwashed clothes. The clothes start giving a strong smell. Wearing unwashed undergarments can be dangerous as it can lead to rashes and fungal infections. Even socks should be washed after a long day's use.

Generally speaking the above remedies and precautions may be enough to drive away your body odour. But in spite of these simple measures if your body odour still exists, it is time to visit your doctor to find out if there is anything more serious to it as strong body odour may be symptoms of some underlying disease and the sooner this is treated, the better it is.

HAIR

Hair is the crowning glory of every individual. A good crown of hair makes a person look much better. But if hair is not maintained, it starts falling and thinning rapidly. Hair once lost is gone forever, hence it is important to look after your hair.

Hair needs to be washed with a good shampoo at least twice a week in a country like ours. Unwashed hair will also lead to a bad odour. It is necessary to oil your hair once a week before washing as the follicles will then get the necessary lubrication and nutrition. Excessive use of shampoo without oiling will lead to a dry scalp and hairfall.

Ladies with long hair should brush it regularly with a soft brush in order to increase the blood circulation in the follicles as well as to keep the hair fall under control. If you need to colour your hair it is a good idea to conduct a sensitivity test before applying it.

It is important to rememberm that unclean and unwashed hair will lead to lice, dandruff, etc., leading to other severe problems including hair loss, bacterial and fungal infections and so on. Hence, maintaining cleanliness of hair is important in more ways than one.

Body hair: A man with an untrimmed beard or moustache gives an unkempt impression and soon begins to look like a vagabond. Similarly, hair sprouting from ears, nostrils, eyebrows, etc., must be trimmed regularly for proper grooming. There are many cases of people growing hair in their ears. Their logic can never be understood as all it needs is a mirror and a good pair of scissors to trim the same.

Nowadays, it has become a fashion for male celebrities to have a clean shaven chest and body. This has caught on to the 'metrosexuals' who do likewise. This is not necessary, as body hair on men is acceptable. Of course, many really hairy men have medicals problems due to excess hair on their chest, back, etc., and needs to be removed.

For ladies, body hair is an unwanted sight and any good beauty saloon will assist in this part of personal grooming. Not only you will look and feel good, it will help you to maintain personal hygiene.

DRESSING SENSE

The first impression of an individual is how he/she looks and what he/she is wearing. We are born with our looks and physical features, thus, not much can be done about this. But we can surely make ourselves look presentable and without too much of an effort. In order to look good it is not necessary to wear Allen Solly shirts or Nike shoes, it is simply a matter of choosing the right right clothes and wearing them confidently.

Do not follow fashion trends blindly: People have a habit of blindly following the latest fashion trends. Here, it is necessary to take a reality check and see whether the latest trend is suiting you or not. Your physical attributes should help you in deciding what to wear. The latest trends may look good on celebrities and models but may not necessarily on you. People who blindly follow others end up wearing wrong clothes.

Simplicity is be the best option: For everyday wear, it is better to go the simple way. While fashionable clothes are suitable for occasions, simple attire is more comfortable for the daily grind. It is not necessary to spend a fortune on clothes meant for daily wear, but it is necessary to have a good choice and go for what suits you the best. Brand names are always unnecessarily expensive, thus, it is better to avoid brand names, unless you are selecting clothes for special occasions.

Footwear: Footwear is an integral part of our dress and thus attention must be paid to what footwear to wear. Here, again it is not necessary to go for brand names as these may be prohibitively expensive. Shoes and other kinds of footwear need should be comfortable since you will be wearing them for the better part of the day. Oversized shoes or undersized ones will give you a lot of trouble. So it is better to take time and select the right size rather than regret later.

ETIQUETTE, MANNERS AND BEHAVIOUR

Etiquette is all about carrying yourself in public. It is a mix of manners and decorum. Proper etiquette is necessary whether in the office or at home. A person without etiquette comes across as boorish and will be generally disliked. Thus, it is necessary to make a conscious effort to behave politely at all times, with everyone.

Most of us behave very nicely with strangers, with our bosses and with people we meet occasionally. But when it comes to dealing with our family members, our colleagues and others whom we meet everyday, we forget to be on our best behaviour. We tend to take those closest to us for granted. There is an old saying *'Familiarity breeds contempt'*. This is very true as we often forget to treat people closest to us with the same courtesy and consideration they deserve.

Office etiquette

In the workplace there are strict codes of conduct. While it is up to the individual to decide whether to follow them or not, it definitely has an impact on how you will be viewed in the office by your juniors, colleagues and seniors. In fact, it will not be far off the mark to suggest that your etiquette may have a bearing when the time comes for appraisal, promotions, etc. It is advisable to keep the following points in mind.

1. Arrive at the workplace or for meetings on time. Punctuality shows your etiquette and regard for others. A person who is late for work puts undue pressure on his colleagues. Similarly, your arriving late for meetings shows scant regard for others who may have to had wait for you.

2. Do not whine, criticise or backbite in the office. This gives out negative vibes and may lead to lack of motivation. It is always better to take a positive outlook on life and stay happy with whatever you are doing.

3. Do not indulge in undue gossip while in office. This is a waste of your time as well as that of the person with whom you are gossiping. Similarly, do not waste your time discussing delicate topics such as, religion, politics, etc. Nothing comes out of such fruitless discussions except that you end up antagonising people. Keep your views to yourself unless asked for. Even when asked for, give neutral answers without hurting the sentiments of others. Never get into heated arguments and long drawn discussions about any controversial topics.

4. Be courteous and friendly to all but do not be overbearing. No one likes a colleague who is extra friendly to the point of intruding into

others' lives. Give people the space they need and get friendly only if they reciprocate.

5. Be polite to everybody including office boys, receptionists, etc. They may be junior to you, but they too are worthy of your respect. Don't forget to say 'thank you' and 'please' whenever required. Show appreciation whenever possible.

6. Never pry into others' desk, drawers, files, computers, e-mails, purses, wallets, mobiles, etc. This is seen as an invasion of privacy and will not be tolerated anywhere. Everybody respects their own privacy and you also need to respect the privacy of your colleagues and friends.

The fact that personal grooming is gaining importance in corporate circles is borne out by the fact that the Hindu group Business Line organised a lecture on 'Personal grooming and etiquette' for MBA students of the Sri Devi Institute of Technology at Kenjar near Mangalore on May 7, 2010.

The speakers highlighted the role of personal grooming and etiquette in the growth of a person in the corporate sector. Presenting oneself and the way you interact and network with other people determines your success in the corporate world. Highlighting the values of etiquette, they concluded that it helps build better relationships, and presents the person positively in a corporate environment. In short, etiquette was termed as a huge asset and a passport for success.

Home Etiquette: The same code of conduct is valid at home also, where mutual love and respect should be shown to all family members. The home and the family is the shelter for all its members and should therefore be a pleasant and safe place where all the members can live peacefully and comfortably. No member must imagine that he or she is the fulcrum around which the home revolves, everybody is equally important at home.

"Don't reserve your best behaviour for special occasions. You can't have two sets of manners, two social codes – one for those you admire and want to impress, another for those whom you consider unimportant. You must be the same to all people."

—Lillian Eichler Watson

***

LAST WORDS

It is good to have an end to a journey; but it is the journey that matters, in the end. - Anonymous.

The management of life is as interesting as it is difficult. One who manages life in the right manner will enjoy the blessings of a good life for a long time. Health, wealth, happiness are all there for us to enjoy, only if we realise their potential, respect their values and do not abuse them.

It is very easy for us to start life on the wrong track and end up losing everything we had. Mismanagement of life leads to a confused and frustrated state which is of no use to any one and the person leads a miserable life. Life is beautiful and like all beautiful things need to be looked after.

Each of the chapter enumerated above are important to managing one's life. I hope the reader will be able to enhance the quality of his/her life by reading and following them.

***